YOU CAN'T MAKE THIS SH!T UP

YOU CAN'T MAKE THIS SH!T UP

STORIES OF A BADASS LIFE

STEPHANIE GELLER

Precocity Press

Editors: Sara Volle and Julie Simpson
Creative Director: Susan Shankin
Cover Design and Illustrations: Tim Kummerow
Book Design and Layout: Andrea Reider
Author Photo: Michelle Vance
Precocity Press, Los Angeles, CA

This book is a memoir. It reflects the author's present recollections of experiences over time. Some names and characteristics have been changed, some events have been compressed, and some dialogue has been recreated. The book was not intended to hurt anyone. The publisher and author regret any unintentional harm resulting from the publishing and marketing of *You Can't Make This Sh!t Up.*

ISBN: 979-8-9892043-7-3 (Paperback)
ISBN: 979-8-9892043-9-7 (Hardcover)
ISBN: 979-8-9892043-8-0 (eBook)

Library of Congress Control Number: 2023923298
First edition printed in the United States of America

This book is dedicated to all the "me's" out there.
The ones that lived it, are going to live it,
and those who wished they had.
It's never too late.

CONTENTS

PART 6: *Just Give a Fuck*

INTRODUCTION

I get asked why I'm writing a book. *I'm not writing a book,* I say. *I'm just telling my stories.*

I had been planning on writing some of these stories for a long time. Since high school, my best friend Samantha and I used to joke about me actually putting them into a book. When she died too soon I decided it was time to commit. So here we are.

Reading this book is not going to change your life. That's bullshit. You were born with everything you need to know. You just have to acknowledge it. Own it. Maybe these stories will help you do that.

People and moments are the only things that can change your life.

I was the free lunch kid. The Air Force brat. The middle child. I was the athlete. The gymnast. The cheerleader. The Waffle House waitress. The telemarketer. The collections agent. Then the executive. Wife. Ex-wife. Lover. Friend. Business owner. And a lot in between.

And now I'm an author. My stories are of love and lessons, being poor, being rich. Of being naïve and trusting my gut. Having fun along the way and rocking it every day.

This book is about believing in yourself and never giving up on who you are. And it's all over the place. Because I am. We all are. Just own it.

I'm not a fiction writer. You can't make this shit up. These are the real stories of what I have lived, my badass life.

PART 1

CARRY YOUR HEART WITH YOU

EDDIE SPAGHETTI

I have always thought of Eddie as my first boyfriend. It was 1970 in Germany. We were five years old. My dad was stationed at Hahn Air Base, a small base up in the mountains. I remember just a few things about living there. The green countryside dotted with castles and hills and tiny white flowers. The heavenly smell of German bread; nothing like the Wonder bread I was used to eating.

Things were bad between the Americans and the Germans at that time. The politics affected everyone. I could feel the tension. There were sit-ins and demonstrations. Not just between the locals and military families. There was also race-related friction between the Americans on base. The runway was a typical spot for activity. People would stand on the tarmac with protest signs. Peace signs. It was a time of flag burning.

The US government was building a beautiful Olympic-sized pool for the German nationals off base. There were no parks and no pools for military families. When we first got to

Hahn, there was no base housing available. We moved into a small place in a village nearby.

There was an older lady who lived across the street who would wave at us whenever we were coming or going. She had a cherry tree and a garden in the front of her cottage. She wore a headscarf, long skirts, and mismatched tops. She used to babysit me and my sisters when my mom ran errands.

Die Wache the kinder? my mom would ask in broken German before dropping us off.

"Ice cream?" the neighbor would ask in something close to English. American ice cream was a treat for the Germans.

Mom went to the commissary on base for grocery shopping, usually for food for the next month. And ice cream. Chocolate if they had it, or vanilla.

Our German neighbor would drape cherries over our ears to look like earrings. We would listen to stories as we shelled peas from her garden. The stories were about her son. Or maybe a cow. I was learning German one story at a time.

After about a year we moved into base housing. It felt like a ghetto compared to the village. Nasty old apartments from the war. Barracks. Green. Dirty. Building after building, all exactly alike. We were packed in like sardines.

There was an empty lot between two sets of buildings where the kids gathered together to play kickball. It was mostly boys, just a few girls. I was small but tough. I was never the last one picked. That's how I met Eddie. Unlike the other boys, he didn't mind the girls playing pick-up games. He was part Italian. And so cute. I called him Eddie Spaghetti. He became my best friend.

As the summer ended, we started school on the base. First grade. Eddie and I were in the same class. Jackpot! We had an American teacher, the wife of one of the soldiers. One day we had a substitute teacher. She was German. Tall, muscular, stern. On that day we happened to have a fire drill. All the teachers marched their classes out in a single file line to stand in the yard.

"Be quiet," the substitute barked at me harshly. "Stop talking in line."

It wasn't me who was talking, but she sure thought it was. She came up and slapped me so hard I hit the ground. Then I wet my pants. I picked myself up and got back in line. I could feel the sting of a nasty red mark on my face. I was sent to the principal and my mom had to pick me up. I wouldn't talk about what happened.

I was too terrified and humiliated to go back to school. I wouldn't even go outside to play. I just couldn't. After about a week Eddie came by to see me. Somehow he convinced me to come back. He was almost pleading with me. He assured me I would be okay. Our regular teacher was back. Everyone missed me.

Eddie's dad was base commander. Which means he was in charge. The German substitute teacher was never seen in school again.

So many of the other military families traveled while they were stationed in Europe, including Eddie, his older sister, and their parents. His family would go camping, or to Switzerland or France, or to the zoo. They would often invite me to join them for weekend trips. I would dream about what it would be like to get to see the things Eddie got to see — but my parents always had a reason not to let me go.

At almost six, I was the kid who saved her Christmas and birthday money from Grandma. I never bought frivolous things; I wouldn't even lend money to my sisters when they asked. But when Eddie's birthday came up I knew that I was ready to spend my money. I had saved every penny.

There were so many Americans around that most of the shops took US dollars. I had $7.00 to buy a present for Eddie. A small fortune. It was all the money I had. I shopped diligently for the perfect gift and ended up selecting a woodworking set. It was $8.25.

"I only have seven dollars," I told the shopkeeper. He looked at my mom. My mom would not give me the extra dollar and change I needed.

"I will clean or do whatever to cover the rest," I promised the man at the store in my limited German. I made the gesture of sweeping and dusting.

"Meine wort ist gut," I said in the best German I could. The man let me have the woodworking set for seven dollars. He told me it had just gone on sale.

I was so excited to give Eddie my gift at his birthday party. I could hardly wait.

"Here's your present, Eddie," I announced proudly as soon as I arrived. All the boys wow'd my gift. I was clearly one of the cool girls.

My birthday came around a few months later.

"Here's your present, Stephanie," he said. It was a baby doll, dressed in pink. It was so delicate and pretty. It's over fifty years later and I still have that doll. It's in the toy box my sisters and I got for Christmas one year in Germany: light wood with hand-painted figures.

Then one day Eddie was just gone. The military had evacuated his family. The nationals hated us Americans, hated the US government. As base commander, Eddie's dad and family were in danger. My mom told me that the family was being threatened to be killed. They left in the middle of the night.

I missed him desperately. He was my best friend in this place of constant uncertainty. I wondered where he ended up.

A good base or a crappy one? What were his friends like? Did he have a friend like me?

My time in Germany taught me what it looks like to fearlessly embrace a new place. How to find home wherever you are. It set the foundation for the person I am today. Kids can be mean and harsh. Adults can be even worse. Together, Eddie and I learned about friendship, caring about others, and what it means to have a heart.

It wasn't the same after he left. I had other friends, but no one like Eddie. Like him, I would soon go to a new base, a new school, meet new friends. But I'd never forget Eddie Spaghetti.

ORDERS

Air Force kids are like free agents:
they can get traded at any time.

I spent my childhood as an Air Force brat. You got to a base that you liked, you would be there for two years. If you got to a place that you hated, you'd be there for two years. You just carried your heart with you.

"We've got orders," my dad would come home and say. And then our lives would change again. You would start packing your stuff right away. You only had a few weeks to be out of your home. Orders could come at any given moment. You got used to the feeling of knowing any day could be your last day in that town.

Edwards Air Force Base in California was a desert. I have a photo of me in a bikini as a toddler watering a cactus. Randolph AFB in San Antonio, I don't even remember. Our tour of duty to Homestead in Florida, near Miami, was a short stint.

And then there was Malmstrom AFB in Great Falls, Montana. Beautiful big sky, just like the license plates say. Part of the Rocky Mountains. Genuinely friendly people. I was in fifth grade.

I met Scooter on the school bus. His real name was Terence, but everyone called him Scooter. When I first noticed him, he had to sit in the front seat because he got in trouble. Now he was allowed to sit in the back again. I sat in the back on the way home from school too. Scooter had a magnifying glass and was burning ants on the seat. He was so cool. Strawberry blond hair and freckles.

"If you like me, you could get off at my stop and walk me home," I teased.

It became our regular routine. We sat next to each other on the bus almost every day.

Then my dad got orders for Thailand, a place families couldn't go. It would be a year, maybe two. Whenever my dad got stationed overseas, we ended up in North Dakota near where my grandparents lived. I wanted to stay in Montana more than anything.

The next day Scooter knew something was different.

"I know that look," he said as I got on the bus. "It's orders, isn't it?"

HOW GYMNASTICS
SAVED MY LIFE

*F*ast forward a few years. My dad was back from Thailand and stationed at Eglin AFB in the Florida Panhandle. I was thirteen and my life revolved around gymnastics. I trained seven days a week. I read every issue of *International Gymnast* magazine. I had pictures on my wall of the great gymnasts. Olga Korbut. Bart Conner. Kurt Thomas. I dreamed about competing in the Olympics.

On the second day of eighth grade I got called to the principal's office. My mom was there to pick me up. When we got home there was a moving truck in the driveway and all our stuff was packed inside it. My dad was on a temporary duty assignment in Texas. We were leaving him for good and going back to North Dakota.

We had no money. We moved into a crumbling apartment complex filled with drug addicts and prostitutes in downtown Minot. I helped clean the building so we could eat. Wiped down the banisters. Collected the lint from the laundry room. In the winter I shoveled snow. Anything for a few dollars.

When we arrived in North Dakota it was midweek and the school year had already started. My sisters and I were all at different schools. Elementary. Junior high. High school. My mom checked me in at the junior high. All the other eighth graders were dressed in mismatched clothes. The vice principal explained that it was "fun week." I didn't get the memo.

"Does your daughter play sports?" the VP asked my mom.

"Yes, she's a gymnast."

"We don't really have a gymnastics team," he said. "But I can send her to the high school for an evaluation."

"We also need to set her up with free lunches," my mom said. Free lunch kids had to go to the office every Monday morning to get a blue card. The cafeteria lady would holepunch your card after you picked up your food. Everyone knew who the free lunch kids were.

The VP made arrangements for me to work out with the high school gymnastics team. I immediately made the varsity team even though I was only in the eighth grade.

That made things look a little more promising.

The other kids were not very receptive to a girl from Florida. I got plenty of the "you're not from around here" looks. And word had spread quickly that I was on the gymnastics team at the high school. That didn't make me any more popular. I didn't understand jealousy at that age. I was a poor kid living in a crack house. Pretending like everything was OK was my protection. But it also made me a target.

My second day at my new school, a girl I didn't know slapped me hard in the face. That was the start of the bullying. She was tall and skinny and wore blue-tinted glasses. Apparently, her boyfriend "looked" at me in home room. But you can't get in trouble if you play sports. It gets you kicked off the team. So I didn't hit her back even though I could have easily leveled her.

My younger sister hated her school. She was experiencing the same things that I was. We were outsiders.

My older sister seemed pleased with the high school. It ran like a college. You could take up to eight classes per day to graduate early. Start early or start late. It had a huge pool with regulation diving boards. I came to find out there was an indoor track and weight room too. It was only a couple blocks from the junior high. It became my sanctuary.

A couple months after I arrived, there was a school-wide fitness challenge over two days. Sit-ups. I could do those — and did 100 in a minute. Pull-ups until everyone else fell. Crossed the rings. Ran sprints.

I not only beat the girls, I beat most of the boys. I set six records. I think I still hold some records. I was strong, both physically and mentally. And determined.

A few weeks later Patricia, the assistant gymnastics coach, saw me walking to practice early one morning in the snow. She pulled over. It was negative ten degrees.

"You *walk* to practice?" she asked.

"Uh. Yeah. Like how else would I get there?"

"Hop in." Patricia was young and had a quiet manner about her. She was the "good guy" coach.

I was the best on the team. Lucky #13. The other girls on the team treated me okay, but there was no one I would call a friend.

"Why don't you take private lessons?" she asked.

"Not going to happen," I said, knowing we couldn't afford it. "I get free lunch."

A couple weeks later our team was competing at home in a dual meet against a team from out of town. I was an all-around gymnast, which meant I competed in all four events.

I had a good meet. My routines were different from those of the locals. Mine had been choreographed in Florida by an ex-gymnast. She was a beautiful dancer and was great with music. Her mother owned a ballet studio, so we had access to mirrored space to create and practice.

My floor routine music was the theme song from *American Bandstand*.

After the meet, the owner and coach at the only private gym in Minot came to talk to me. Scott. He was passionate about the sport. He had a great energy about him.

"You are very good," Coach Scott said. "Why don't you work out at my gym? I have classes, lessons, and a show team that performs all over the area."

"We can't afford it," I explained to him. "The high school team is free."

After practice the next Monday, Patricia pulled me aside. It was about the private lessons and classes I knew I couldn't afford.

"Coach Scott would like you to stop by the gym this afternoon if you can," she said. "I can drop you off."

My mom was there when I got to the gym. It was state of the art. All new equipment to work out on. Spotless clean. It even had a small shop.

Coach Scott explained that I had an anonymous sponsor.

"A what?" I asked. I had never heard of that. My "sponsor" would be paying all my expenses for lessons, classes, and travel to shows. I would be provided with leotards and footies to practice in.

"What's the catch?" my mother asked suspiciously.

"There is none," Scott said. "I don't know who it is and neither will you."

From then on I would go to the gym for private lessons at 6:00 a.m. I would work out for a good hour or so and then go to school. I didn't go to regular P.E. Most days I went to the high school to practice in the middle of the day and then went back to class.

I ran almost every day. Weight training four days a week. I was the perfect size and body type. At one point my body fat was nine percent. With little coaching, I would just learn every day. I would do my routines over and over again. Try new tricks. Put the music on and try to perfect my routines. Walk off the pain. Put baby ointment on the blisters.

Sometimes I would show up to the gym and there would be new workout clothes or a warm-up suit for me left by my sponsor. They would pay for the special outfit for the travel team to perform in. Whoever they were.

"Can I help out here at the gym?" I would ask Coach Scott. "Maybe clean up, maybe put some of the equipment away?" I would offer. I guess I just didn't understand why someone would do that for me.

"No, go get something to eat, get some rest. Tomorrow is another day," was always his answer.

Then I would walk home. Do as much homework as I could based on my exhaustion level. Eat something, although food was often scarce. I came to appreciate those free lunches.

I would always leave thank you notes. With Coach Scott I tried my best to say how much I appreciated everything anyone did for me.

To this day I don't know who paid all the bills. I suspect it was either Scott or Patricia. Or both. I am not sure how to even begin to say how much of an impact it had on my life.

By the end of the school year we were headed back to Florida. I wasn't sad to leave the school part. Or the living conditions. Or the bullying. Or the freezing cold. But I would miss Scott's gym. I loved to compete, even when I didn't win. People believed in me. I learned to believe in me.

"1980 Olympic team, you better make it," Coach Scott told me as we said our goodbyes.

HOW GYMNASTICS ALMOST ENDED MY LIFE

Life is not fair. Accept that. What counts is what you choose to do with the hand you are dealt.

I started ninth grade back in the Panhandle. Niceville. Yes, that's a place. I had grown up a lot. I was tough. I was strong. Every time you move, you get a chance to reinvent yourself. You can be whoever you want.

I knew who I was. I was a gymnast who was going to be in the Olympics.

That ended when I busted my right ankle. It was hurting me a lot so I went to a doctor and he took x-rays. He said it was just a sprain. I slept with an ice bag taped to my ankle every night for a month. It didn't get better. My mom took me to a different doctor on duty. It was broken. That doctor pulled the original x-rays and said it had been broken for at least six weeks; I had been training on it that way. Now I had a nasty cyst on my ankle. The size of a half dollar. The doctor said I may not walk right.

"I am going to compete again," I told the doctor. "You *fix it*." I cried when I said that to him. I can still feel the tears running down my face. My mom sat in the corner with her arms crossed, an odd look on her face. She was miserable and now I was too. My life was over.

The doctor drained the cyst with the biggest needle I had ever seen. It hurt to the point that I screamed in pain. He hadn't told me it was going to hurt like that. It was so bad I thought I would pass out from the pain. It was so bad the nurse left the room.

The doctor put me in a plaster cast. I trained in it. I couldn't run, but I did weights. I did flex training at the gym. I wasn't willing to have my dream die. I had college scouts looking at me.

But I couldn't recover. No matter how hard I tried. The pain from the break and the cyst wouldn't go away. They shot my ankle up with steroids. Three times. It burned like putting your hand on a hot stove.

I still don't have much feeling in that ankle. But I do rock five-inch heels with no problem.

My gymnastics dream was over. That was my ticket out of this life. My ace. And it was gone.

My life felt like it had ended. I would fantasize about swallowing an entire bottle of pills and just going to sleep. My ankle hurt. My heart hurt. My heart was broken. I didn't know how to live another day. *Who am I now?* I wondered over and over again.

My friends convinced me to try out as a cheerleader for the high school JV team. Pam and Rebekka. They were junior high cheerleaders and popular. I thought cheerleaders were wanna-be athletes. But I had to find a replacement for gymnastics. I no longer had a winning hand but I wasn't ready to fold.

Tryouts were during the summer before school started. The cheerleaders were selected by a panel of judges made up of teachers and coaches, and the results were taped to the school door the next day.

I made the squad. My new life was beginning.

PART 2

I Don't Know How to Be Anyone But Me

SIX TEENAGERS AND
AN EL CAMINO

There's a reason the Florida Panhandle is known as the Redneck Riviera. There's no denying the beauty of the white sand and emerald clear water, but as far as the people go it's basically as if you took Alabama and put it on the beach.

By junior year I was one of the cool kids. High school football was the biggest thing in town and I was a cheerleader. Niceville had no major sports teams, professional or college.

There were also no concerts for "big name" bands in town. You had to drive to Biloxi, Mississippi or New Orleans to see any bands, or festivals, or anything really. Biloxi was three hours away. NOLA was a little over four.

At that time most shows had festival seating. General admission and no assigned seats. It was a free-for-all. Hot, sweaty, smelly — and filled with multiple varieties of smoke. Virtually no security.

When the doors opened everyone would rush the stage and squish to the front. The floor was nasty. And your feet were going to get stepped on. Make sure you pee before you get situated because there is no going back.

The band Foreigner was playing in Biloxi. We took off in my best friend Samantha's El Camino. Me, Samantha, and four guys I didn't know — they were Samantha's friends. I had cute pink Converse high-top sneakers. It was a sunny afternoon.

We got there in time to hang out, tailgating in the parking lot. Smoked cigarettes. Had a few drinks in the back of the El Camino. Blared the car radio as loud as we could. All the other cars were doing the same. We headed into the concert. You didn't really want to get separated from the group.

This concert, we actually had seats. The cheap seats, but seats nonetheless. I threw up onto the floor of our row. "EWWWW," one of the guys yelled out.

We moved down a couple of rows. Thankfully there were seats available.

When the show was over it was time to make the long drive home. It was a school night. School was gonna suck, but the rule at my house was no matter how late you come home you have to go to school the next day.

Good luck getting out of the parking lot. We were heading there when it started to drizzle. Then it started to rain. We squeezed three of us in the front and the other three squeezed up against the window in the open bed in the back. We figured it would only last a bit. One of those quick showers. Nope. It kept raining. It was pouring.

No one had jackets. Then we learned we had no windshield wipers. Well, we had wipers, they just didn't work.

"We can't drive like this," one of the guys yelled. "I can't see anything. We need wipers." "Everyone take the shoelaces out of your shoes," I suggested. "Tie them to the wipers. Bring them in to us through the cracked window. Pull right, pull left. Right. Left."

It worked. We made it home safely. Everyone was soaked. Hungover and exhausted, we wore our Foreigner T-shirts and sunglasses to school the next day. We were the cool kids who made it to the concert. And made it back.

GOOD, BAD, AND PRETTY

G rad Night is when thousands of teenagers from all over the East Coast flock to Orlando for an all-nighter at Disney World. What could possibly go wrong? As the year came to a close the teachers prepared by compiling a list of kids to keep an eye on that night. Apparently I got put on the "blacklist."

I was the kid who got in trouble for leaving school grounds to go get lunch for me and my friends. Muffaletta sandwich for us to share. So good. The shop in town did a great job recreating the NOLA favorite. Salami. Ham. Mozzarella and provolone. Topped with olive giardiniera. Cut in four pie-shaped pieces.

I got in trouble for smoking in the bathroom. There was one bathroom where everyone went to smoke Marlboro Lights between classes. Then there was the whole food fight that broke out in the cafeteria. I'm not sure who threw the mashed potatoes first. I don't know how I got blamed for that one. But I was one of the five that had to clean it up.

When you got in trouble in 1983 your choices were suspension, detention, or a paddling.

I took the paddle. I reported to the office wearing my cheerleading uniform.

"Turn around and put your hands on the wall," the vice principal directed me. "You will get three hits on your butt."

I did as instructed. And stuck my ass out a little extra, more than necessary.

"Just go," he said, "or I will call your parents." By then I didn't really have parents. I was crashing at Samantha's house until I could figure out how to get my own place.

"Call all you want," I said defiantly. "I don't even live at home." He pointed to the door.

"Wait, do I still get to sign the paddle?" I asked. Taking a sharpie and writing your name on the paddle was part of the rite of passage.

So it probably made sense I was on the bad kid list, even if I had a 3.8 GPA and was a student aide to three teachers.

Grad Night arrived. I showed up late to catch the bus. I had to sit in the front since it was the only seat left. It was going to be a long six-hour bus ride so I brought my pillow. It had a zipper to adjust it to how hard or soft you wanted it to be. It also held a small bottle of rum perfectly. When I accidentally dropped my pillow it landed on the floor of the bus with a thud. Oops.

One of the girls had to pee. Like really pee. They stopped the bus. So much for my nap. I bought a soda from the vending machine at the rest stop and had the rum in my purse. Time to make a drink.

We finally got to Orlando in time to check into our hotel and change. I came out wearing a miniskirt and short T-shirt with turquoise blue polka dots and Chinese characters on it. Five-inch high heels with bobby socks.

"Unacceptable." One of the teachers stopped me as I got ready to board the bus.

"But I'm not the only one wearing a miniskirt," I protested.

"This is a dress-up event," the teacher said.

"I *am* dressed up," I insisted.

"You have two choices: change or don't get on the bus."

I switched into light blue pants with black polka dots; the pants were so tight the teacher probably regretted asking me to change. I left the heels on.

The park was closed except for seniors from different cities as far away as NYC. The girls were dressed in everything from shorts to prom dresses. The guys in everything from suits to shorts.

I had a joint in my pants, so my friends and I got stoned in the bathroom. The event went from midnight to 4:00 a.m. There were greasy food trucks and about a dozen bands on four different stages. Emerging punk and cover bands doing dance and rock hits.

After the event closed down, we had to find our bus among the hordes and then head back to the hotel. Sleep for a few hours until we had to catch the bus early in the morning for the dreaded ride home.

I slept the whole way back to Niceville. Again, sitting in the front of the bus. Only now with no rum.

LUNCH CLASS

In high school I felt like I lived in a parallel universe. Between waitressing at the Waffle House and a job at the mall I worked at least 30 hours a week. Sometimes more. My mom tried to kill herself and then spent a month in a psych ward. Another time she got arrested and spent a weekend in jail for breaking into her third ex-husband's house. He was the volunteer chief of police and a real creep. She said she only married him so we could have air conditioning over the summer. My younger sister ran away.

When I got my class schedule for my junior year it was the usual stuff. Trig, AP English, Spanish. I got stuck with a history class that had lunch in the middle of it. That meant class for 20 minutes then lunch for 20 minutes then class for 20 minutes. Starting at 10:30 in the morning.

It was a nightmare for teachers to have middle lunch. You get started, then lunch. Sometimes, kids don't come back.

I had Coach Wilson for history. He was one of the football coaches. Young and shy. He had taught my driver's ed class the summer before.

The first day, everyone filed into history class. It was me and a bunch of my friends. Denzel, Grace, Saul, and Sonja. There was also a group of stoners.

"Is this for real?" Coach Wilson exclaimed. "How could *all of you* end up in one class?"

"Just lucky?" I said under my breath.

One day on my way to lunch I ran into Tim, one of the cute baseball players, a pitcher. He was a senior. Probably not the brightest one on the team, but cute enough to hang out with. He invited me to join him outside. Why not?

We headed to the area where all the stoners hung out, between our school and the junior high. We sat in his junky old car and talked about baseball. And college. He admitted he wasn't good enough to pitch in college. We talked about going to school and why it sucked.

I had a cigarette. His car had about four inches of water on the floorboard of the back seat. With garbage floating in it. Leftover food wrappers, and cups from fast food. Toilet paper. I kept thinking, *this is kind of weird*. He saw me staring.

"There's probably a fish or two back there," he joked.

"Shit," I said, "I need to get back to class." But when I looked at the time it was too late. So I just went to my next class.

The next day Coach Wilson confronted me.

"Miss Geller, what happened yesterday? You missed the second half of class."

"I was in the ladies room," I said without missing a beat. "I was having a . . . female situation."

He visibly blushed. There were snickers from the stoners. They probably saw me hanging out with Tim, but they damn sure weren't going to say anything.

Works every time. We all have to put up with a lot in this world but if you are smart you learn early how to find your people and get out of a sticky situation.

BLUEBERRIES

Speaking of sticky situations, to this day I can't stand the smell of waffles. Regular waffles, pecan waffles, peanut butter waffles. Blueberry waffles are the worst. At Waffle House the blueberry waffle was a mound of pie filling on top of a waffle with whipped cream.

I got my driver's license the day I turned sixteen. Passed the test in my mom's powder blue nine-passenger station wagon. That same day I started my job at the Waffle House in Shalimar, a one-stoplight town in between Niceville and Fort Walton Beach. I worked the night shift. Nine p.m. till seven a.m. As waitresses we had to clean the bathrooms and wash the dishes. For $2.10 an hour plus tips. The cooks took out the trash. That was code for going out back and getting stoned.

By 3:00 a.m. the drunks had fallen asleep at the table. That meant on top of their blueberry waffles. Never pretty. The part you had to worry about was what if they suck a blueberry up their nose. That was gonna be a problem. You'd prop them up, clean them up a little and lay them down in the booth. Until they woke up or you woke them up. It depended on how busy it was and if you needed the booth. We never called the cops.

The one sheriff in Shalimar came in for coffee every morning around 5:00 a.m. I always had it ready for him.

"Breakfast today?" I would ask. He usually just had coffee. Black. I knew all the regulars' orders. How they liked their eggs. Whether they liked grits or hash browns or took their iced tea sweet or unsweetened.

And then there were the children. If I filled in during the day, it meant getting to the shop at 6:45 a.m. Families would come in. Order waffles. And more waffles.

Whenever a kid ordered the blueberry waffle I would cringe inside.

"Excellent choice," I'd say with a smile. I worked for tips.

Later I'd be cleaning blueberries off the ceiling.

"How exactly did the blueberries get up there?" I'd ask the other waitress.

"Not sure. Tall kid?"

Blueberries in the booth, on the table, the floor, the windows. All that, I could understand. But the ceiling? There were no busboys at Waffle House. Grab a broom, a towel, some cleaner and stand on the table. Yep, I got this.

"Don't mind me, I'm just cleaning blueberries off the ceiling," I would tell the occasional person staring at me.

The drunks were easier to clean up after. The drunks were also better tippers. Maybe they appreciated how we'd make sure they didn't snort up a damn blueberry.

In the mornings, my shift would end at 7:00 a.m. when everything, including the dishes, was done. It was my 5:00 p.m. So I would eat dinner — a burger or a chili cheeseburger. Maybe the BLT with cheese. Occasionally I would have the custom omelet that I created. Sausage, onion, tomato, with cheese melted in. You could smell the sausage and onions as they cooked on the grill. I would sit at the bar as the waitress called in my order.

"Two scrambled. Sausage, onion, and tomato out like an omelet. Wheat. Hash browns." It was cheaper than ordering an actual omelet. We only got $3.50 as a food allowance after a shift.

At seventeen you could go home after an all-night shift, throw on a bikini, pick up some cheap pink wine at 7-Eleven and head to the beach. Wash the smell of waffles off in the ocean. I would call and wake up my friends.

"C'mon!" I'd say over the phone. "I only have a few hours before I have to get home and sleep. I'll pick up the Blue Nun."

GRITS

No one can teach you attitude or work ethic.

My older sister started working at the Waffle House three years before I did. People would never guess that we were related. She was blonde with blue eyes. I had auburn hair and hazel eyes. She was reserved. I was a little more wild.

Looks aside, though, we shared the same attitude and work ethic, so we made a great team. We worked the night shift together for over a year before she went off to college in Pensacola. We would swap out customers or double up if we thought we would get a better tip.

Along with a couple of scholarships, my sister paid her way through college with that job. She went on to become a high school teacher, administrator, and counselor for thirty years.

Teaching at twenty-four, she looked so young she was mistaken for a student. "Can I see your hall pass?" a veteran teacher asked her one day. "I'm the AP history teacher," she replied, smiling.

About grits. The way I feel about blueberries is the way my sister feels about grits. She still hates grits. I still hate blueberries. The problem was the same: drunks passing out in them. Make sure they don't inhale them. All in a night's work.

Any given night a loud fight could break out in the parking lot. Usually between a few of the regulars. Nothing would solve that better than yelling out the door: "Hey, your burgers are done. You want them to get cold? *Cut that shit out.*" Food. That always did the trick.

The best part was around 4:30 a.m. That's when the late night crowd and the early breakfast crowd collided. Bartenders and strippers would come in for eggs, bacon, and grits at the same time the morning coffee drinkers and the cops would start to roll in. The strippers came from over the bridge to pick up their to-go orders. They rarely ate in the restaurant. But they always had cash and tipped well.

The looks between these groups were priceless. Freshly showered tourists and locals in their jeans and shorts. The night crowd still in their "walk of shame" outfits and last night's party dresses. We made sure everyone felt welcome. Treated everyone with respect. Didn't make assumptions.

One morning a couple of the girls walked in from a long night's work wearing nothing but oversized T-shirts and strappy platform heels. No pants. No panties. They lined up at the cash register next to the morning crowd waiting on coffee.

In the '80s Waffle House only took cash. There was one register that got balanced after every shift. The strippers usually paid in ones.

Some of the early birds had clearly never seen a stripper. Their jaws dropped. For us, it was just another Saturday night. Or rather Sunday morning. When the men looked to anywhere near the register, their wives would glare at them. The leftover drunks would make smart-ass comments.

"How much?" they'd ask.

We would give them the "look" that said *not cool here.*

An older couple once told my sister that we should update our "No shirt, no shoes, no service" sign to include pants and panties.

Around that time I also worked at the mall for a designer men's clothing store. *Two Guys Menswear.* The owner would go to Italy to buy the merchandise. Trendy styles. Mostly upscale suits, ties, and shirts with French cuffs. But we also sold authentic parachute pants that ran $125 a pair and funky graphic shirts that looked like either a five-year-old or Jackson Pollock had splattered paint on them.

One day a short guy came in, probably in his fifties. Dressed in jeans and a T-shirt. He wanted leather pants.

"Yes, we've got those," I said. "They look good in the black. But you should have the beige too. I'll measure and have them hemmed for you."

So I was on my knees making sure they would hang exactly right. Leather pants ran $300 a pair. We spent an hour shopping for other items for him to buy. I just listened more than talked.

He picked out a shirt on his own.

"Oh no, no, that is bad." I laughed.

"Really?"

"Yeah, try this on."

He looked at me and said, "I like you."

He ended up buying four pairs of leather pants. Three shirts. And a pair of shoes. I did more sales in that hour than I typically did in an entire week.

I hadn't noticed until I rang him up that his bracelet said O$KAR in diamonds. Big diamonds. Yes, the S was a dollar sign. He was none other than Oskar Church, the guy who owned every liquor store in the county. Every license. Almost every club, including the gentlemen's club where the strippers worked.

Oskar would only buy from me from then on. I was just doing my job, just being me.

During those years I learned that money is money. No one's cash is greener than anyone else's. People are people. What's up to you is how you let them treat you and how you treat them.

Please, just don't inhale the grits.

REGGIE PART ONE

The cook and I started dating. I used the $50 I won in the steak and egg contest to ask Reggie out to dinner.

The steak and egg contest was all about who got the most in steak and egg sales. Not exactly a bestseller at the Waffle House. I'd make all my regulars order the steak and eggs or steak and hash browns. They both counted. Whether they wanted it or not I would convince them to order it.

"Don't you want me to win the contest?" I'd ask when the diners wanted to order something else. They'd reluctantly order the steak. I would smile and assure them they could have their regular order next time.

That usually did it.

I was sixteen and Reggie was eighteen. We'd go out dancing on our nights off. Usually at Victor's in Ft. Walton Beach. It was an old airplane hangar and basically two bars in one with a massive dance floor. They played all the great hits. Duran Duran. Flock of Seagulls. Madonna. Even punk. On a busy night there were easily fifteen people working behind the bar.

It didn't matter that Reggie and I were underage. Most of the bouncers and bartenders were Waffle House regulars. We'd always get a heads up before the raids.

"Tomorrow night don't come in any time before eleven. The cops should be gone by then."

"Gotcha."

Reggie and I worked night shifts together. When it was slow we would make up recipes at 3:00 a.m. Cookies in the microwave. Mix the bacon and sausage together and put it in the waffle batter. We would play dominoes and backgammon.

You learn a lot about someone in the middle of the night in winter with no customers for hours. Reggie was a bit of an oddball. Dry sense of humor. Loved to talk shit. Not exactly a warm and fuzzy personality. He had a dark side. I knew things no one else knew. How his older brother was the only son his dad wanted. His parents never accepted Reggie for being different. His older brother was a jock. Reggie was anything but.

"Burgher boys play sports," his father would say. And worse.

After dating for two years, everyone thought we would get engaged. Including his parents. I think they were grateful he had a girlfriend.

The holidays came around.

"I bought you something special for Christmas," he told me as we sat on the swings in the park near where we both lived. It was on the water in front of an old mansion where Al Capone used to hide out.

"I got you something too," I told him.

I'd bought him a beautiful watch. Well, beautiful for what I could afford. I always put money away. And now I could show Reggie how much I cared about him.

The holidays were hectic for both of us so we planned to exchange Christmas gifts on New Year's Eve. I had to work that night so we met in the park before my shift. He unwrapped the watch and his eyes met mine. I had a sinking pit in my stomach. Whatever was coming next wasn't going to be good.

His special gift to me was a ceramic vase. A vase? I was devastated. A fucking vase. I felt unloved and stupid beyond words. I thought it would be jewelry. Maybe even an engagement ring. Then he told me he couldn't be my boyfriend anymore. But we could be friends.

"What the hell is going on?" I demanded. "I just want the truth," I said. "But hurry up, I have to get to work."

"You know I love you," he said. "But you also gotta know I'm gay. If I ever wanted to be with a woman, it would be you."

I was hurt but I wasn't shocked. There was always something "off" about Reggie. I was young and inexperienced but not a virgin.

"I don't know what to say," I said. "But if you are done, I really need to get to work. Happy fucking New Year."

I was beside myself when I showed up for my shift. I sucked it up and put on a brave face. I would only cry in the bathroom. Wipe my tears and go take care of our customers. My gay boyfriend was not their problem. Definitely not on NYE.

Reggie was true to his word. We stayed friends.

He continued to struggle with relationships the rest of his life. There was no way around it. I loved him to death but Reggie was hard to like. He used to ask me, even decades later, "Why do I have to tie a pork chop around my neck to get people to play with me?"

What could I say? He was just so angry. He had a hard time getting over things. Blamed everyone but himself for his problems. He was a glass half empty kinda guy. Sometimes his glass didn't even have water in it. I was the opposite. But somehow we couldn't help loving each other for exactly who we were.

NOT MY DESTINY

At the end of high school most kids get ready to head off to college. That wasn't in the cards for me. I had the ACT and SAT scores, the grades, and the activities to go. I got accepted to every college I applied to, including Penn State, USM, and LSU. A lot of my classmates were heading to FSU in Tallahassee or UF in Gainesville, so I was definitely not going to either of those. I wanted to be as far away as possible from what had been my life.

But I had no guidance on *how* to go. Neither of my parents had graduated from college. I was already living on my own and had no money for college. I wasn't at risk enough or good enough to get attention from any high school guidance counselors. I simply fell through the cracks. I didn't know what resources could have been available to me.

I'm sure I could have figured it out, but I guess part of me didn't want to go. Or didn't want it badly enough. When I know I want something, there is no changing my mind.

In August of 1983, three months after graduation, I was about to start my shift at the mall. I parked my car and walked across the warm asphalt toward the beige double doors that made up the main entrance. Before I went in I stared at those doors and had an overwhelming feeling that I just couldn't do this anymore. Any of it. Tears welled up from somewhere deep inside my being. *This is not who I'm supposed to be. I can't keep doing this. I just can't.*

Something had to give. I didn't know what I wanted, but I knew what I didn't want.

That night I went home to the apartment I shared with my then boyfriend, who would eventually become husband #1. He had been at the beach all day drinking beer, getting stoned, and playing frisbee. Just another day in paradise.

"I can't stay here," I announced.

"Why?" he asked, confused. "It's great here."

"Great? What, with our dead-end jobs, hanging at the beach?"

He still looked confused.

"I want more," I said. "I've decided I'm getting out of here. Soon. You can join me or not."

"OK, well, where?" he asked.

"I don't know. Anywhere. Anywhere would be better than this."

We settled on LA. He had caught up with two childhood friends he knew from outside of Boston, where he grew up. They were living in LA and loving it.

"We can stay with my buddy until we get a place," he said.

So it was decided. We gave notice at our jobs and our apartment. Rented a U-Haul with a tow for the car. Started packing up the place. Our shag sofa, TV, a queen-size bed and a dresser, some stereo equipment and a few pots and pans. Two weeks after my meltdown and epiphany at the mall we were on the road to Los Angeles with our cat and all our stuff.

I can't say exactly what brought me to the breaking point. It's something I have inside of me that just knows when to say "when."

I am all about trying. Fearlessly trying. Never do anything half-ass. If you try halfway in gymnastics you end up with a broken bone or worse. I don't know what my life would have been like if I'd gone to college in Pennsylvania or New Orleans. But I do know I wouldn't be where I am today had I been too afraid to pack up all my shit and take a risk that summer after high school.

HOT DOGS WITH THE BOSS

Los Angeles was a huge change from my small town in Florida. It is a big pond.

After stints selling typewriter ribbon and working at a bank I got the opportunity to interview at a small equipment leasing company that was expanding in the LA market. At the time Reggie was working for them in Atlanta. That's how I got the interview.

I took a bus to the interview because my car — a 1972 poop-brown Mustang — broke down. They were still moving into the new office so I interviewed sitting on an overturned crate. *This isn't good,* I thought.

I got hired two days later as the assistant to the assistant. I had never worked for a "big" small company. This felt like an opportunity. Learning from the ground up.

Peter, the owner and founder of the company, came from Boston to visit us. He wanted to meet the new people and speak with the team.

The office manager asked me to take Peter to lunch. I was broke. I couldn't take him anywhere in my car that may or may not start. Sometimes you just need to be a little creative.

"It's a nice day," I said to him with a smile. "Let's take a walk. You can leave your jacket."

We walked about a block or two to one of my favorite cheap restaurants. Happy Dogs. Yes, it was a hot dog stand. A small, funky place that had an old-fashioned diner feel. White with red and black accents and a couple stools in front. A few small tables with chairs near the back. We ordered at the counter and picked a spot looking onto the street. Two dogs for him, one for me. A coke for him and a water for me.

"Don't you want fries?" I asked. "Onion rings?" We opted to share fries.

I prayed my credit card would go through.

We talked about the office. My role and how I was doing. My background. I was honest, but didn't let myself get too far into the weeds. We talked about the company he built. What I wanted for my future. We talked about careers and life stuff. He was a nice man with an easy smile and bright eyes.

As we walked back to the office he told me something I will never forget.

"I will teach you whatever you want to learn," he said.

HOT DOGS

"I know I have a lot I want to learn," I said, "but I'm not sure exactly what it is."

"That's okay," he said. "You don't have to have it all figured out. I just know you want to be successful. I can tell."

When we got back to the office the manager asked how our lunch went.

"I think it went well," I said. "We walked down to Happy Dogs."

"You did *what?!*" she exclaimed. "You know you get to expense the lunch."

I was baffled. I didn't know I was supposed to take him to the Ritz or somewhere swanky. I'm sure he's been taken to fancy lunches all over the country. But how many times has he walked to a hot dog stand?

I was broke and my car was broken down. I was just working with what I had. And it left a lasting impression. I honestly don't know how to be anyone else but me.

NOT EVERYONE GETS A TROPHY

REGGIE PART TWO

If your glass is half full, it's also half empty.
What would make it full?

Reggie was stuck. Never had a boss he liked. Took everything personally. He would have a job he liked for a bit and then he would end up quitting.

He was living in Atlanta and got a great job. He bought a fabulous condo in the midtown area just outside the beltway. It was stylish. Beautifully decorated. Fireplace. Loft. Guest room. He got into a relationship. He was happy — at least for Reggie.

Then the boyfriend broke up with him. It felt sudden to Reggie. He didn't understand. He never had closure, kept asking why. He never got over it.

He decided to quit his job and become a massage therapist. Went to school to get his certification. He tried working at a spa. Hated it. He didn't like the way they did things. He said they folded the towels wrong. No one got coffee or water fast enough for the customers. On and on. Reggie never worked well with others.

He decided he wanted to buy this house in a neighborhood that was transitioning. Open his own massage business there. Cater to other gay men who wanted a more private experience. You get the picture.

He got a realtor to sell his condo and had an offer in a couple of weeks. It came in a couple thousand dollars under asking. He called me, furious.

"What's wrong?" I asked. He could barely speak.

"I got an offer on the condo but you'll never believe this. It was under by two thousand."

"That's totally normal," I assured him. "Sellers go a little high. Buyers offer a little less. You meet in the middle."

He wasn't having any of this.

"Well, I'm insulted. I'm not going to sell it to her now."

"Are you out of your mind?" I asked, frustrated. "It is a great offer. Don't take it personally. Counteroffer. That's normal too."

By this time he was already set on buying the other place.

"Think about it," I continued, in my best financial advisor voice. "TVM. Time value of money. If you don't take the offer, then you keep paying the mortgage and the insurance and everything else. Every month you don't sell you are incurring costs. That two thousand is covered in one month. And now you have a second mortgage."

It was 2006. The no-doc loans that started in 2005 were one of the worst ideas ever. To buyers, to bankers, to investors. It would all come crashing down a few years later. For Reggie, the crash came sooner.

"Do. Not. Do. It," I pleaded. "This ends badly."

"I'll get another offer on the condo," he said confidently.

He never got another offer. Got foreclosed on.

I visited him at the new house. He had set up a massage table in the guestroom. He set up a website for his massage "business."

"You know," I said, "most people would never go into someone's house to get a massage."

"My clientele will," he assured me.

It was a creepy house. It looked like a place where your crazy grandma would live. Antique furniture. Doilies everywhere.

At first, his business was doing pretty well. "Fresh meat." But that didn't last long.

He hated his neighbors. It was a rough area, even in daylight. Reggie's yard flooded every time it rained. He was sure the neighbors were doing it on purpose. Never mind the fact that he was at the bottom of a big hill. Everyone was out to get him.

Foreclosure #2. Drop the keys at the bank.

Reggie decided that he didn't like Atlanta anymore. I remember thinking, *Yep, Atlanta is the problem.*

Reggie had two Springer Spaniels. Scout and Molly. He decided they liked to camp. Like for a long time. Like *living* in an RV.

"Huh?" I said when he told me his plan. "You're going to get an RV and just cruise around from park to park?"

"Yeah, there are plenty of free parks," he assured me. "I can map them out. Pretty much all my stuff is in storage anyway."

"Maybe just take a month and try it out first," I advised him. "Camping for a few days is very different from *living* in a campground. You know that, right?"

Next thing I know he's calling me again.

"I found a used RV with a pull-out that's not too expensive."

"Hmm." I knew what was coming next. I told him hell no, I wasn't going to lend him the money or cosign his loan.

"Rent an RV," I said. "See how you like it. It's really not the same as a weekend getaway." He didn't listen.

He managed to figure something out. And off he went in his used RV with the two dogs.

It was a lot harder than he thought. First, you need reservations. He didn't know that. The "free" campsites are not so nice. They don't have showers, laundry, and pools like the fee parks. Some of them didn't allow dogs. I told him all this when he called early on, but he didn't listen.

He found a camp that he liked on a lake somewhere between Atlanta and the Carolinas. He made a couple of friends there. They helped with getting supplies and watched out for each other.

Not long into that stay, Molly started acting weird. She died right there in his arms. That changed everything.

"I am so sorry, Reggie," I said when I heard the news. "I know how much you loved her. She was a great doggie." There was no consoling him. His Springer Spaniels were the family that loved him. It was the only unconditional love he ever felt. I could feel his heart breaking.

  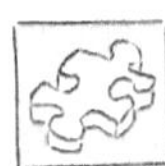

Reggie decided that Minneapolis would be a good place to move to. It had an active gay community. The weather is good. He hated the heat in the South. Off he went.

He got a one-bedroom apartment about a block from the baseball stadium. A little dated. Nearby bars and restaurants. Young people.

He set up the massage table in the living room. He got clients once again. Fresh meat.

He didn't like the building manager. Scout peed in the elevator.

He called me one day out of the blue.

"I need a favor," he said. "I need you to come out here. You are my power of attorney, remember?"

"Okay...?"

"I'm really sick and the doctors can't figure it out. I'm in the hospital. Not sure for how long."

"Let me check flights and call my office," I said. "I can be out there tomorrow."

This is where being a frequent flier pays off. Cost doesn't matter, you use your points. You know exactly how to search for the flight you need.

Reggie gave me instructions on how to get to his place.

"Take the train from the airport to the ballpark," he said. "My place is right across the street. The manager will have a key for you. The dog needs to go out three times a day. She gets one bowl of food and fresh water."

His apartment was filthy. I took the dog out. I have never had a dog but I figured it out. Leash. Walk. Poop bags. Put your hand in the bag, pick up the poop and then turn the bag inside out. Tie it up and put it in the garbage bin. Try not to gag.

I went to the hospital. He was still awake. Heavily medicated. Hooked up to all sorts of machines.

"Make me a promise," he said. "If I am not off the ventilator in five days, you will pull the plug. I don't want to be a vegetable."

"Sure. You will be fine. We got this."

I stopped the doctor on my way out.

"What does he have?" I asked. "What is going on?"

"We don't know yet. Has he been to the Amazon or some other country recently?"

Well fuck me, that doesn't sound good, I thought.

The next few days were all the same. Walk. Hospital. Walk. Hospital. Talk to the doctor. Go to the apartment. Walk. Pick up poop. Seeing someone in that condition rips your heart out. I am not sure how I kept it together. I did the laundry. I cleaned the house. I checked in with my office.

On the third day, I ran into a couple from the building.

"Are you new here?" they asked.

"No, I'm dog- and house-sitting for my friend. Do you know Reggie? He's in the hospital."

"We don't. But you look tired. Can we buy you a drink?"

"Absolutely."

It was day five. Time to face the music, as they say.

"Okay, Doc," I inquired at the hospital, "where are we at? You heard what he asked me to do."

"He is getting better, but it's going to take a little longer."

"Are we talking days or weeks or months?"

"I don't know exactly. My guess is days but it depends on how he keeps responding."

I needed a minute. I went to the lobby and put my head in my hands.

If I pull the plug, he dies. If I wait a few more days and give him a chance, I break my promise. If he dies, he won't know the difference. If he survives, he can be pissed off at me for all I care.

I went to the doctor and said we were going to continue the treatment.

Back to the routine.

Day nine came. The doctor wanted to talk to me.

"We are about to take him off the meds and the ventilator and see how he responds."

When I saw him next he was typical Reggie.

"What day is it?" he asked.

"Does it matter? You are alive. Doggie is good."

"What happened to my tooth?"

They had knocked off a veneer taking out the ventilator.

"You broke the promise," he said.

"Yes, I did. And I would do it again."

As soon as I took him home to his apartment, he told me to leave.

He had left me in charge of his life but didn't need me anymore. I booked a flight for the next day. My head hurt. My heart hurt. But it's not personal. Reggie was just being Reggie.

Some people celebrate life. Some people are simply enduring it. Just don't expect a trophy for showing up for a friend when they need it the most.

LOSING CAN BE WINNING

I know nothing about kids. I am a great parent to my cat. I first met my nephew Aaron when he was two months old. My sister was exhausted and needed a break. She was scared to death to let me watch him while she took a shower.

"Well, he weighed over nine pounds when he was born, so he'll probably just bounce," I assured her. She didn't think that was funny.

While she was in the bathroom, I just walked around with the baby and watched CNBC reporting on the stock market. I explained to my nephew how important investing was, and what happened that day in the market.

She came out to a happy baby snuggled on my collarbone. She was in shock

"We're cool," I said. "Take a break. Take a nap. I got this — as long as he doesn't poop."

The years passed by fast. At eight years old my nephew was still the only child in the family. I lived ten hours away by car but we kept in touch.

"How did Aaron's soccer tournament go?" I asked my sister.

"Good," she said nonchalantly.

"Did they win? Did he score any goals?" I was all excited to hear about the tournament. And how Aaron played.

"Well, they don't keep score," she said matter-of-factly.

"Wait, what? Then what the hell is the point?" I was confused. "What do you mean, they don't keep score?"

"Every kid has to get a trophy."

By this point I was pretty worked up. "Life is gonna suck for them," I said. "Real life doesn't work that way. Do the parents and coaches actually think the kids are not smart enough to figure out who won the game?"

I was nine years old the first time I competed as a gymnast. My mom wouldn't go, saying she would be too nervous. The truth is she was on the verge of some kind of mental breakdown.

I walked in to the tournament and there were three trophies. First, second, and third place. Gold, silver, and bronze. Just like the Olympics. I knew wanted to win the gold. I had

14
5
3
12
14

never actually competed in a tournament like this before. Heck, I had never even seen a place this big. A table of judges. I had no idea how it all worked. My coach had to explain it to me.

During warm-ups, I noticed there was one girl that had a back handspring, and I didn't have one in my floor routine yet.

It's okay, I'm still better, I told myself.

I won the gold. The trophy was all of six inches tall, an eagle with wings. I still have that little trophy, even with a broken wing that I had to superglue back on. That trophy meant I was a winner.

Children and adults need to "play" to win. They also need to know how to lose and do it with grace and respect. And learn from it.

After that gymnastics meet my coach invited me to come to the Olympic Training Camp.

"She's too young," my parents told the coach.

But that was a lie. We didn't have the money.

A couple years after Aaron's soccer tournament, he had the chance to go to an away basketball camp.

"I don't know if it's a good idea," my sister said. "He's so young."

I didn't have to think about my response.

"I had the chance taken from me," I said. "Please don't do that to him. He's a good kid, let him go. It will be a great experience. And even if it's not a great experience, it'll be something he'll always remember."

She still didn't seem convinced. So I challenged her last excuse.

"If it's the money," I said, "I will help."

He went to camp and had a great time. They even kept score at the games. He grew to be 6' 4" and made the varsity basketball team in tenth grade.

My only child may be a cat, but I know a thing or two about pushing yourself, competing in life, and not letting opportunities pass you by.

SOMETIMES WINNING IS WINNING

My fortieth birthday was an opportunity to throw the party that most people dream about. I wanted to celebrate my way. By the end of my thirties I had a successful career, a 5,000 sq. ft. home in an upscale neighborhood a block from the ocean in Boca Raton, and a cute second husband. And I looked damn good for turning forty, if I might say so.

I told husband #2 what I wanted for my birthday in great detail.

"Are you *sure* this is what you want?" he asked, surprised.

"Yes," I said firmly. "My AMEX concierge service can help you with all the details."

I had decided on a private jet to the Bahamas. For dinner. It was close enough to go there and back in one night.

Looking at the planes was so exciting. They were all spectacular. We investigated schedules, cost, how many people each plane would hold, the interiors, and the layout of the seating. Every detail. Then we picked out the restaurant,

Dune, located in the One & Only Ocean Club, next to the Atlantis Casino on Paradise Island.

I designed and sent out elegant black-and-white invitations. The invitation just included the date, time, and place to meet. *Black tie optional. Passport required. Please RSVP by April 9th.* No other details.

Within days we heard back from everyone. They were all excited about whatever the party was going to be. People made plans to join from near and far.

Reggie flew in from Atlanta. I picked him up from the airport and took him to the house.

"So, what is the party plan?" he pressed me.

"I'm not telling," I said with a smile. "Not even you."

I helped get him settled in for the weekend. His room in the house had double doors onto a balcony and was decorated in creams. Marble-topped dresser and nightstands. Ensuite bathroom. The towels, extra toiletries, hair dryer, hangers were all in place. All the amenities of a five-star hotel. I even made sure there were chocolates by the bed.

"You like?" I asked him with a smirk.

"Geez, Steph, you did all this?"

"I did. I selected every piece down to the matching plant stand."

Once Reggie settled in, he came down to the kitchen. It had a massive onyx island that was open to the family room.

"So what's the plan for tomorrow?" Reggie asked again.

"I'm not telling," I said. It was part of the fun.

My husband went to the bathroom and Reggie looked at me.

"I know the truth," he said.

"What truth?" I grimaced.

But I already knew the answer. I knew what he knew: The party was all being paid for by me. Like always, my husband was just portraying himself as the "rockstar." He got to live the life of a successful businessman, thanks to the Bank of Stephanie. Golf a few days a week. Drive around in a BMW and pick up the dry cleaning.

"It's okay," I shrugged. "At the end of the day I will get the party I want."

Reggie and I set out platters, crystal glasses, china plates, and linens for the next day before calling it a night.

We got started again in the morning after coffee. We set out an ice bucket for champagne. We arranged the platters for the hors d'oeuvres. And the flowers for the table. My husband managed to set up the bar.

Time to get cooking. Gourmet appetizers for everyone as they arrived. Smoked salmon with herb cream cheese topped with capers on pumpernickel, stuffed cucumbers, mini Beef Wellingtons with horseradish mayo. Prosciutto-wrapped melon. A bowl of olives next to the bar. Not to mention caviar with all the accoutrements.

It was time to get ready for the evening. Shower, hair, makeup, and jewelry. I wore a yellow silk gown with a plunging neckline, and criss-cross gold strappy heels. The guests all arrived on time and were dressed for the occasion. The ladies had black cocktail dresses. The men in tuxes or suits.

My husband made sure everyone knew *he* had made the arrangements for my party. He made it sound like he did all this as a gift for me. I just let it go.

The limo pulled up to the driveway and everyone climbed in. We arrived at the executive airport in Boca Raton. That's the exclusive airport for private jets only. No TSA, you just show your passport and wait in the lounge.

You are escorted to the tarmac and to your private jet complete with the red carpet. It was a scene from a Hollywood movie. I felt like Julia Roberts in *Pretty Woman*.

The flight attendant greeted us with a friendly hello as we boarded the plane. Forget first class, this is the only way to fly. White leather seats and couches, lacquered wood tables, and a marble bathroom. Champagne for everyone. The young, sexy blond pilot came out and introduced himself. I looked at Reggie as he looked at the pilot and we both giggled.

After less than 45 minutes flying over a perfectly-timed sunset we landed and were met by two limos. There was a slight breeze, and it was not too hot, even for the men in suits and tuxes. We split into two groups for the short ride to the Ocean Resort for dinner, which my husband made a show of paying for.

When we landed back in Boca, we returned to our house for the afterparty. The bar was still set up and I had glasses ready.

"Anyone need anything?" I asked, "Drink, snack?" *Always the hostess.*

There was a knock at the door. I figured it was the police. No. It was our friend Jon's teenage kids from his first marriage. For some reason Jon had given them the address.

"I am not so sure they should be here," I said to Jon.

"Ah, give 'em a snack," he said.

It was late. I have no idea what time it was when Reggie decided it would be a good idea to give our friend Jack a lap dance on the patio. Jack's girlfriend panicked. She lost it. Jack lost it. Then Reggie really lost it.

Eventually Reggie went upstairs, crying. I went up to check on him. He was having a classic Reggie meltdown, making everything about him.

"Why am I always the bridesmaid and never the bride?"

"It's my fucking birthday," I told him. "You can have your pity party tomorrow."

I woke up early the next morning and took two Advil with coffee. I learned that my sister-in-law and her husband went home to their fancy neighborhood to discover they were locked out of the house. Rather than ruining her new dress and shoes she took off all her clothes before crawling in through the kitchen window. Her prim and proper neighbors must have loved that.

My fortieth was a moment in time that cannot be duplicated. And it included one hell of a party.

It was my party.

COACH

It was 2017. Husband #2 and I had divorced less than two years after my fortieth birthday. I had moved from Florida to Texas. I was still kicking ass in my career and reluctantly decided to start dating again. I'd been texting and talking with a guy I met on Tinder. Everyone called him Coach. He was a high school teacher and baseball coach.

We traded pictures. I took a leap of faith that the pictures were actually him. He was probably thinking the same about me. He was good-looking, tall, and athletic. My type.

As I got to know him, I discovered that for fun he worked on crews for barbecue competitions and festivals. He even crewed for a team at the Houston rodeo with hundreds of teams. The biggest BBQ competition in the country.

It reminded me of how many memories are around food and gatherings. A smell can take you to another place or time.

Coach and I would chat on the phone, so I knew he was at least somewhat real. One night we were talking about food. BBQ specifically.

"Next weekend the BBQ guys are all going to be in St. Louis for the festival," he mentioned. "Some really cool teams. I've crewed for a couple of them in the past."

"Cool," I said. "I love BBQ."

"They call it 'Que in the Lou.' It's not a competition, it's more about the fun. Just six teams cooking for bragging rights. Great dynamic. Music, demos, tastings."

"Wow, sounds like a fun time for sure!"

"Yeah, some of the best of the best will be there. License to Grill. Notorious P.I.G. The Mad Cows. World champions. But I can't go," he said. "Just too much going on, especially with my parents after the hurricane."

I could hear the disappointment in his voice.

Hurricane Harvey had just hit Houston. The devastation was heartbreaking. People lost everything. His parents lost their home, business, everything. All of Houston was exhausted. Everyone was also helping each other in any way they could.

"I'm so sorry," I said. "I got off easy." I lived in a high-rise in River Oaks and never even lost power or cable.

Then I had a thought. "What if there's a way you could go?" I asked him coyly.

"I just can't justify it. I need to use any money to help my parents and everyone who has lost so much."

"Well, I've got nothing special going on this weekend. I have miles and points. We could go." I jumped on the computer and started looking up flights on Southwest as we talked.

"For real?" he asked in disbelief.

"Yep," I said, checking the schedules. "What if we take off Friday morning and come back Sunday afternoon? Can you get out of school?"

"You're crazy."

"I know. But if you're serious I can put this together now. There are good flights available. Direct from Hobby airport, just a two-hour flight. You in?"

He didn't have to think about it too long.

"I'm in."

I booked the flights and a room at the Marriott downtown after asking for his legal name and date of birth. I couldn't just put "Coach" on the reservation.

Now that I had his full name, I immediately googled him. Everything checked out. We agreed to meet at the gate on Friday.

"You'll recognize me," he said. "I'll be the guy in the cowboy hat."

"This is Texas," I reminded him. "You probably won't be the only one. But I do have your pictures."

We found each other at the gate. A quick hug. He was in jeans and boots and a hat. So was I. Neither of us checked any luggage. Easy.

"Bar?" I asked.

"Good idea."

He had a beer and I had a mimosa. Let the fun begin. We boarded the flight separately since I had status and got to go early. The flight was nowhere near full.

I had a white wine on the plane and he had water and snacked on nuts. He admitted he didn't love to fly. I assured him I didn't plan to ever die on a flight.

We landed and grabbed an Uber to head to the hotel. I had guessed right on which Marriott was closest to the venue. I kinda smile inside when I realize how easy us road warriors make travel look.

We checked into the hotel and dropped off our carry-ons. Nice room, one king-sized bed. He didn't blink.

Off we went, walking and talking on the short block-and-a-half jaunt to the venue. It was a nice afternoon, sunny and no humidity.

Friday was set-up day. No attendees. Just the teams prepping. Apparently a good brisket should smoke for twenty hours.

"COACH!!!" the guys yelled as they saw us walking up. Nobody knew he was coming.

"You're here! How?" asked his friend David.

"Where else would I be?" he joked. He introduced me to everyone as his friend Stephanie. "She gave me her points so I could hang with you this weekend."

"How about a drink?" one of the guys from Notorious P.I.G. asked. "Vodka or rum punch?" He pointed to two fifteen-gallon orange Igloo coolers sitting on a table.

"Vodka," I said, thinking, *This is going to be a long day.* The last time I saw a punch like that was high school. The vodka punch was tasty. Not too sweet, a little tangy.

We checked out the other teams and visited his friends.

Some of the booths were pretty straightforward. Tent, grill, table out front, maybe a little decorating. Some went all out. License to Grill had hay bales, pumpkins, sunflowers, even a patio area. One team added a bar. Notorious P.I.G. had a giant inflatable pig.

Most of the teams have a "specialty." The whole pig team. Team Brisket, the rib folks, chicken, sausage. Anything that could be grilled or smoked. Not a salad to be found.

Everyone had a story or two to tell. Intense competition, nightmare trips, broken-down equipment, lost food. One big party. I got adopted into the tight-knit clan pretty quickly.

The next day I offered to help with food prep.

"Can you chop the celery, carrots, and onions?" Debbie, one of the ladies working on the side dishes, asked.

"Absolutely." I helped out with whatever they needed me to do. Coach was working on License to Grill's smoker. Drink in hand.

After a bit, I took a walk and ended up sitting down next to Tommy and a couple of the guys from Notorious P.I.G. Tommy starts telling the story of the night before.

"I went to the Portolet," he said, "and on my way back the cops came up saying they didn't want no homeless around this weekend."

We all laughed.

"I told them I'm the pitmaster for Notorious P.I.G.," he continued, "and they were like 'Sure you are. Did you steal that T-shirt?'"

Tommy was as skinny as a heroin addict. He looked like he had been up for days without showering. Drinking, chain smoking. His jeans were dirty from manning the smoker all day. He did look homeless, but damn he could BBQ.

The crowds started to come around 10:00 a.m. I bet you could smell the food a mile away. Start carving and serving up some Que. One of the local bands started to jam on the small stage across from the booths.

I headed over to one of the cooking demos by License to Grill. I was just standing in the back but one of the helpers didn't show.

"Let Steph help," someone said. So I got to be a sidekick at the demo. Very Vanna White.

After the crowds left around 8:00 p.m., the "real" cooking began. The guys hold back some of the good stuff for the crews.

When someone passed out, and a few always do, the guys would take unflattering pictures and make fun of them the next day. They talked about old times. Coach got caught sleeping in a chair still holding a beer. We all saw the picture the next day.

On Sunday morning, we got coffee and walked down to say our goodbyes to the crew. Long hugs. Everyone was so glad we came.

We headed to the airport, tired as hell but all smiles. Slept on the flight. Parted ways shortly after we got off the plane. I never saw Coach after that.

We didn't really have any chemistry, but we had a great time together. I'll never forget how much fun that weekend was. Wild, sure. Why not? Some of my best memories come from being spontaneous, from not being afraid to say yes or ask that question: *Why not?*

STRANGER DANGER

Still, there are times when *no* may be a better answer than yes. Not all strangers are friendly.

Rewind: One Friday when I was fifteen, my best friend Samantha and I decided to play hooky. She needed a day to hang out. Her parents had just moved to the next town over, Ft. Walton Beach. That meant a new school, the cross-town rival. The move was hard on her. She had pretty much decided to drop out of school at that point.

We opted for her friend Antonio's parents' pizza place. Tony wasn't my favorite person. Samantha dated him on and off. He was dull and boring and I didn't like the way he treated her. He was short and not necessarily attractive but apparently well endowed. I had no desire to find out.

The pizza place was a dump. Looked like a mafia joint. Old red carpet. Smelled like cigarettes, spilled beer, and pepperoni. But we could drink Miller Light and shoot pool for free. Well, not exactly free. We would help Tony by serving customers. One of them was Bobby. He said he was seventeen. He was rough-looking. Skinny. Greasy blond hair, pockmarked skin. Crooked teeth.

"Do you want to go out?" he asked me before leaving the restaurant.

"Okay," I replied. I knew it was a bad idea, but it got me out of the house.

He picked me up at my parents' house in an old green Bronco and we went out to eat. Italian. It was an odd place. It also looked like a mafia joint. After that he convinced me to hang out at his place and "talk." His room was in the basement of a crumbling house. Mattress on the floor and an old TV. We did just talk. Then I insisted he take me home so I didn't miss curfew.

"Can I take you out again?" he asked as I got out of the truck. "Maybe next weekend?"

Since things went okay, I didn't say no. The next weekend he picked me up and wouldn't tell me where we were going. My gut instinct was screaming, *This is not good.*

I was right. He drove through Beasley Park where everyone from my high school hung out. His intent was show me off to my friends. It was god-awful. It was a "slap" for someone from another school to date one of "our girls." It was downright embarrassing.

"I want out of here *now*," I said strongly.

"Why?" he asked, playing dumb.

We left and drove around the corner.

"This isn't working for me," I told him.

"Well, you can't break up with me."

You know you are in trouble pretty fast with a line like that. The look on his face scared me.

We drove around the block and stopped at a red light before a bridge. On the other end of the bridge there was a convenience store.

"Let me out *now*!" I screamed.

That's when he reached under the seat, pulled out a handgun and held it to the side of my head.

"You're going nowhere," he said slowly. "You got that?"

Nothing can prepare you for how to feel in a moment like that. I was thinking fast about how to get out alive. *Do I jump out and make a run for it?* I decided to try and talk my way out, but it didn't work.

"We're going back to Beasley," he insisted.

I thought about jumping out again. *Think, Stephanie, think.*

"Please baby, just take me home. We can talk later."

He drove back to Beasley. That decision probably saved my life. Axel, one of my good friends and a badass football player, walked up to the truck when he saw me.

We had both lived in the same shitty apartments in town and had classes together. I looked at Axel and gave him the side eye. Desperation. He knew something was wrong. Really wrong. He asked Bobby to let me hang out with my friends and they would make sure I got home.

"No," Bobby said point blank. He was pissed off now. He looked down at the gun, which was halfway hidden by his leg. I could see it, but Axel couldn't see from standing outside the jacked-up Bronco.

"Fuck you people." Bobby glared toward my friends.

He sped off in the Bronco with me in it, heading east down a stretch of road where there is nothing but beach. He pulled over, leaned across me to open the passenger door, pushed me out, and sped off.

Thank god. I started walking back toward the park. I should have run. He made a U-turn and came back after me. The gun was visible again.

"I'm going to take you home," he yelled.

"No thanks," I said as I walked more quickly.

"I am not asking you. This is not a choice. Get in the fucking truck."

Not all decisions have the same outcome. He kills me here. Buries my body on the beach. Or I could take my chances and try to sweet-talk my way out. I got back into the truck.

The only way back was past the park again. As luck would have it, Axel noticed. Bobby saw him and freaked out, started to drive crazy. He jumped the curb and hit a tree. A big tree. He went to my side of the Bronco, grabbed me, and violently threw me out of the truck. He pulled me up and began to run down the street, dragging me along.

When we reached a 7-Eleven at the end of the street he just let go of me and took off. I was in shock. Then a dark maroon mustang pulled into the lot. I would know that car anywhere. It was Axel.

"God, are you okay?" he asked.

"I think so."

I was a mess. But I was alive. He drove me home and walked me inside the house.

My mom and stepdad were pissed that I was late. *Late*? They were pissed at Axel. I thanked him profusely for probably saving my life and told him to go home.

"We'll catch up Monday," I said apologetically.

I tried to explain everything I had just been through to my parents. The ride. The gun. The car wreck.

"Aren't you going to call the police?" I asked. "There's a truck wrapped around a tree." I don't think they understood or believed me or cared.

I later learned from a friend of Bobby's that he was fourteen, not seventeen. The Bronco belonged to his friend Rodney. Bobby had a seventeen-year-old girlfriend who "took care of him." They lived in that basement together. Apparently, she was pissed about me and what happened that night.

Samantha and I never talked much about Bobby after that. There really wasn't much to say. Shit happens. Life can and will change in an instant.

A few years later Samantha's sister was murdered outside her own apartment. A girl from our high school was killed on the beach and found not far from where I got tossed out. Another friend got into an argument with customers in a bowling alley he managed and they came back and beat him to death with a baseball bat.

Just another day in the Redneck Riviera. I could have easily been any one of those people.

THE BOMB THREAT

affle Houses are open 24/7, 365 days a year. We never locked the doors. Spring break in the Panhandle was always a little rowdy, especially late at night. The bars didn't close until 4:00 a.m.

I was a senior in high school. I didn't know it at the time, but it would be my last spring break in Niceville. I was supposed to have a rare night off one Friday but they needed a waitress at the Ft. Walton Beach location badly. So I agreed to work. I figured the money would be good. When I got there, the cook was drunk in the back, lying on the counter next to the ice machine. The waitress, Sally, introduced herself. She was missing some teeth and was eight months pregnant with twins.

The crowd was a little rougher than I was used to. Really drunk. Smelled like they had been fishing all day and hadn't showered. I was now the cook, waitress, and hopefully not the EMT. The place was packed.

Each order had a code that was called in to the cook. Nothing was written down. Multiple orders. We are running low on grits, start a pot. Yell at Sally to start some more tea. To hell with the dirty dishes until we need them.

"Two over easy, bacon, scattered and smothered, pecan waffle, sausage," Sally would shout.

"Wake the hell up!" I yelled to the cook. He didn't move, but he was breathing.

I had no one to call for help. I was the help. I'm not a trained cook but I knew the menu inside out. I hit the grill. Those hash browns weren't going to scatter and smother themselves.

A couple of police officers came in around 2:00 a.m. Cops got free coffee so they were Waffle House regulars. I was happy to see them, given the crowd and the night.

"Is there a manager available?" one of the officers asked Sally.

"No, just the cook," she said.

"Can we talk to him?" the other officer asked as he looked around the place. The cooks were almost always men and higher in the pecking order.

"Hmmm, he's passed out drunk in the back," I piped in while flipping over some bacon. "What's going on?"

"Can we talk to you for a minute?" the officer asked me in an oddly hushed tone.

"I don't usually work at this location. I'm filling in."

"Please step over here, ma'am."

This didn't seem good, and I had bacon on the grill.

"There's a bomb threat at the store," the officer whispered to me.

"What?! You gotta be kidding me. Who threatens to bomb a Waffle House?" I said quietly, while keeping an eye on my bacon.

"We need your help to get customers out of the restaurant calmly."

I took inventory of what I was dealing with. A drunk cook, drunk customers, and hopefully not twins on the way from the waitress. To hell with the bacon. I went booth to booth and quietly informed everyone that we needed to exit to the parking lot.

Most of the customers just left without finishing or paying for their meals. After 30 minutes, the place was empty.

The officer came up to me and said, "Well, ma'am, turns out there's no bomb. But we appreciate your assistance."

I was left with dirty tables, no customers, no money to pay for their orders, and no tips. The company policy was that you had to pay if customers skipped on the bill. *Hell no, not tonight,* I thought.

The cook decided to wake up just before the morning shift started to arrive. I was beyond exhausted.

WAFFLE HOUSE

I had never been so happy to see a morning manager.

"It's going to be a long day for you," I said, filling him in on what had happened. "The police said they'd be back this morning."

"See you next time?" he asked.

"Nope. Tell them not to invite me back," I said, totally exasperated. "I'm outta here. But can you make me a BLT with cheese and hash browns? To go, please."

FINDING HOME

You can't put the toothpaste back in the tube.

Home is a place where you can cook and eat whatever you want whenever you want. Cold slice of pizza at 4:00 a.m.? Yes please. Home is a place where *you* get to make the rules. At seventeen I wasn't old enough to sign a lease. But my survival instinct was telling me I had to get out of my mom's house for good. I couldn't sleep on the floor of my friend Samantha's house forever. I needed another place to live.

I had looked into filing for emancipation. Supposedly that would allow me to divorce my parents and essentially become an "adult." It was the law in California. Not in Florida. The person at the courthouse said she had never even heard of it.

My Plan B was to try to live at the low-rent apartment complex where Reggie used to live. I met with the manager of the complex. I was lucky; someone had just been evicted.

"You need fifteen references and I will give you a place," the manager told me that Monday morning.

"No problem," I said. "I'll be back on Wednesday."

I'm sure she never expected to hear from me again.

I went to my bosses at the Waffle House. I went to the teachers at my school. I used Samantha's mom. Reggie. My sister and a couple of her friends. The shoe guy from the mall, who I occasionally stayed with. The sheriff I always had coffee ready for in the morning. Pretty much anyone I could think of and a few more. Everyone agreed to vouch for me.

I returned to the manager on Wednesday morning. "Here are my fifteen references to get an apartment. When can I move in? I have the first month's rent and the deposit."

"I have a one-bedroom on the first floor."

"Perfect," I said.

She gave me the rules and the rental contract and showed me around. Where the garbage went, where the washer and dryer were located, where to park.

I called in to school "sick" that next Monday. It was my day off at Waffle House. My shift ended at 7:00 a.m. It was moving day!

I got this, I thought.

When my mom went to work, Samantha and I snuck into the house and took my bed and dresser and the rest of my clothes. She had the El Camino, so we could get the cheap furniture to my new home.

My older sister was getting a new couch, so she gave me her old couch. She even had her friend drop it off to me. It was butt ugly. Blue and green flowers. It matched the green shag carpeting in the living room and the harvest gold kitchen.

When I returned to school the next day, my teachers had boxes for me. Filled with pots and pans. Dishes. Silverware. Towels. A blanket. A blender.

The manager at the Waffle House let me know there were some items that were going to be "replaced." Plates. Cups. A frying pan. I could have them if I wanted.

I knew I would spend my new-found adulthood looking for ways to extend this kind of generosity to people who deserve a break in life. And I did, whether it was taking a chance and hiring someone who didn't have the perfect resumé, standing up for my nephew, or never hesitating to say thank you. I had learned early on the power of kindness.

I never stayed another night at my mother's house. That game was over. I didn't get a trophy, but I won. Once I left, I knew I wouldn't go back. My apartment was full of used furniture and mismatched dishes but it was *my* house.

I had a home. I felt like the luckiest person in the world.

PART 4

LOVE WITH YOUR WHOLE HEART

THE HOTEL ROOM

In the summer of 2009, I was freshly divorced and had been living in my new condo in Boca. I went back to visit the Panhandle of Florida for the Fourth of July. I had been talking and texting with this guy from high school, Frankie, since my last visit.

Gotta love those points for airlines and hotels. Travel for free. Throw a couple bikinis and shorts and a sundress into a bag. Packed and ready to go.

"Is there a plan?" I messaged Frankie when I got there.

"Not sure, but Baytown usually has something going on," he replied.

"Great, let's catch up with Samantha there."

Frankie seemed disappointed but agreed to make it more than just the two of us. Frankie and Samantha tolerated each only because they were both my friends.

Off we went out to the Baytown area. Shorts and flip flops. Baytown has the better shops; nice bars and restaurants open to the deck-type walking area.

We hit a few of the outside bars and walked around. I wasn't loving the vibe. It was crawling with tourists, mostly drunk and sunburned from a day of fishing on the sandbar. Bands playing bad covers. Weak overpriced sugary drinks designed for tourists. We hung out until the fireworks were over and then headed back to the hotel.

We decided to put Samantha in a shopping cart and push her around the hotel parking lot. It was a nice night. The beach, a breeze. The smell of the ocean. We were in our forties but could still have fun like teenagers.

It was getting late. Samantha went home. Frankie and I headed upstairs to my hotel room. It didn't take long before we got into a huge argument. About sex — or the lack thereof. There had been so much conversation about sex on the phone since we reconnected. He said he had been curious about me since high school. *It's going to be amazing,* he'd brag to me. But when it actually came down to it that night, he was too drunk to deliver.

I threatened to go to the lobby. "I'm sure I can find a friend to buy me a drink," I said. That pissed him off.

The fight turned loud — yelling, screaming. That got the other guests' attention. Someone must have called the police. By the time they showed up I was passed out in bed wearing only a bra and pink thong panties. I was dead to the world.

When I'm asleep like that, good luck waking me up. Frankie managed, though, by shaking me until I finally came to life, of sorts.

"Whaaat? What the hell is going on?" I asked in my sleepy daze.

"The police want to talk to you," Frankie said. He was wearing just shorts and no shirt.

I walked to the door in my panties and bra. The police had kept the door cracked open to observe while Frankie tried to wake me. They had to be thinking I was a dead body.

"Yeah, we had an argument," I told them. "Yes, I am fine. Can I go back to sleep now?"

"We don't want to hear anything else about you two again," the officers warned us. "We do and someone is going to jail."

We didn't end up in jail. At least not that night.

TEQUILA

That Fourth of July weekend wasn't the only time a night with me, Samantha, and Frankie ended up with a visit from the cops. Frankie and I dated on and off long distance for years. He'd visit me in Boca or we'd connect whenever I'd go back to the Panhandle.

One time Samantha met us for drinks at a local Mexican place. That can only mean margaritas and tequila shots. Go big or go home.

We decided to go back to Samantha's to make steak sandwiches and a pasta salad. Stopped at a store to pick up food to grill. More tequila.

Frankie was already a little hammered. Us girls were fine. We made the pasta salad and marinade for the steak. Threw in a little tequila, Worcestershire, lemon, hot sauce, whatever we could find.

Samantha and I had a blast as we cooked, listened to music, and just "girl talked."

"I can't believe he's so drunk," I giggled quietly to Samantha.

"I know, what a lightweight."

"We need to get him something to eat."

"I'll fire up the grill," Samantha agreed.

Frankie decided he was the "grill master" and went outside to cook the steaks.

"Thank god," we said to each other. *Just get him out of here.*

As we were doing our thing, he was in and out of the house and overheard us talking about the guy she had been dating, and some of the red flags. He decided to get on the computer and look him up. The internet is ugly.

I was in the kitchen and didn't hear the whole conversation, but it wasn't good. Frankie just kept talking shit about Samantha's boyfriend. She was at the end of her rope.

Samantha came back into the kitchen. Frankie brought the steaks in. They were beyond overcooked. So much for being a master griller.

We decided to make him a plate, hoping something to eat would help his attitude. Samantha dropped a piece of steak on the floor.

"Fuck it, he won't know, just rinse it off and throw it on a bun with some cheese," I said. "He's being an asshole."

I went to the bathroom to pee. I came out and he was heading for the door with a ripped shirt and no shoes.

I looked over at Samantha. I couldn't believe what I saw. She was holding a gun in her hands. Apparently she had fired it at his feet while I was in the bathroom. I hadn't heard a thing.

"What the hell happened?" I asked her. I was in total confusion. "I went to pee. Pee. Good grief."

"That asshole hit me in the head!" she yelled at me.

She'd grabbed him after he hit her and that's how his shirt got ripped. Chaos. Don't know how the gun came into it.

Wait. Everyone, slow down a minute.

I sat with her and made sure she was okay. Her anger turned into tears.

The neighbors must have called the cops when they heard the gunshot, because the next thing you know they were at the front door.

"You have to file a report," the police said.

Samantha was fine with that. The cops asked me questions too.

"What am I supposed to say?" I asked. "We were hanging out and I went to the bathroom. That's all I got."

SECRET LOVER
PART ONE

I was a disaster after divorcing husband #2. If Frankie was everything I *didn't* need at that time, Bertrand was the opposite. He was exactly what I needed at the time I needed him. I had been through a lot. I was beat up.

We worked for the same company but he was on another team. We were in Chicago for sales meetings and our teams would be working together in the future. I was the National Sales Manager, so I ran the meeting. That meant scheduling all the speakers, deciding on the agenda, and coordinating the executives to speak to the team. Every meal. And the entertainment. For three and a half days.

This meeting, I had made arrangements for all of us to go to a bar that had pool tables and karaoke with a live band. They had roped off an area for just us. My team arrived first. They knew my rule about being late. We had just finished up the day's meetings so we went straight to the bar.

The team Bertrand worked on came in a bit later. They had changed into jeans and shirts. He walked in and I was immediately like, *Wow*. He was drop-dead gorgeous.

I had the company credit card, so the drinks flowed. Everyone went wild for the karaoke. Bertrand and I met at the bar to get drinks. Started talking. Discovered we both lived in South Florida. I gave him my card. Then I had to do manager duty. Make sure everyone was having fun and staying in check to some degree.

It started to get late, and I had only booked the space for us for so long. Most of my team knew it was time to go. I have a rule about not being out past 11:00 p.m. on work trips. Everyone on my team knew about my eleven o'clock rule. Our first meeting the next day was at 8:30 a.m., which meant 8:00 for me.

A text from Bertrand woke me up at 1:30 a.m. His crew was still out partying. He wanted me to come to meet him. Then he offered to come to my room. It was tempting, but I knew it was a bad idea. Still, it confirmed the attraction was mutual. But I already knew that.

Both teams were at the first meeting the next morning. Bertrand and I exchanged stolen looks and smiles. I loved knowing he'd been texting me just a few hours before.

When we got back to Florida, Bertrand and my buddy AJ agreed on meeting up with me for happy hour. Then AJ bailed, so it was going to be just us.

I decided to buy a new dress to look pretty for Bertrand. Happy hour turned out to be dinner. I moved from my side of the table to sit next to him. I rubbed my leg against his. We kissed.

Then we went to a dive bar. Sat on the counter talking and laughing about music and bands and everything and nothing.

We ended up at the beach. The sun would be rising soon. We lounged on the sand in beach chairs. Then I crashed at his place. Just crashed. It was the best first date.

He texted me the next night. "What are you doing?" he asked.

"Meeting friends and heading to the Irish Pub at Mizner. I think there's a band tonight."

"Can I come?"

I didn't hesitate. "Sure."

Mizner Park was a block and a half from my place in downtown Boca. Near all the bars and restaurants and beautiful shops. We spent the night drinking car bombs and dancing and smoking cigarettes we bought from the bar. Bertrand fit right in with my friends.

The next morning we decided brunch would be a good idea. But first coffee. Then Advil.

Off to brunch, sitting at the bar. I prefer sitting at the bar. Too many years of traveling alone.

Nice couple sitting next to us. "How long have you guys been together?" they asked. "You are so cute."

"Since yesterday," I said.

Bertrand would sit next to me at my kitchen table as we were both on conference calls with our teams at the same time, alternating going on and off mute. We were still a secret except to a few friends. We were not sure how that might go down with the company.

It was the kind of fun and attraction where we pulled into the garage and didn't make it into the house. Bent over the back of the car having sex. Then walked in, poured a glass of wine, and made some dinner. Or got dinner. It didn't matter, we just winged it. Spent hours laughing. We both loved politics, the market, sports — him baseball, me football. Good food and wine. After my marriage ended, this was exactly what I needed. Excitement. Desire. Fun. No stress.

Bertrand and I didn't have a fairytale ending. What we have is better. A friendship that's still amazing year after year.

SECRET LOVER
PART TWO

was sitting in the Crown Room, Delta's lounge in the Atlanta airport, on my way home from ... somewhere; honestly, you are so exhausted that you forget sometimes. Especially if you've been to several cities in just one week.

I was snacking on cheese and having a glass of Cabernet. Not a great wine, but free. Always leave a good tip. Waffle House taught me that.

Frequent fliers don't want to sit out at the gate with the regular folks. The lounges have more space to work, and it's quieter. The bathrooms are nicer. Airport lounges are usually full of road warriors.

I sent Bertrand a text: "Where you at?"

As a road warrior that was a common question. You run into people in strange places. I have woken up at home and had to look around and be, *Oh, home.*

"Just landed at ATL for a dinner meeting. You?" was his quick response.

"Crown Room ATL. Got a bit of time to kill before my flight home."

"Miss the flight," he shot back. "I'm staying tonight at the Marriott across the street. Stay with me."

It was a tempting offer. I went to the gate and asked the agent about changing the flight. They said it would cost $600.

"What if instead . . . I miss my flight?" I asked the gate agent.

"We'll rebook you. No charge."

So I sat there as they paged my name and closed the plane door. I watched the gate agent watch me. Perfectly legal. I missed the flight, right at the gate. Once they shut the door, I walked up smiling and rebooked for the morning flight. For free.

Bertrand had to do drinks/dinner with clients at the hotel.

We had a plan. I took the airport shuttle to the Marriott. He had left me a key at reception. I had to walk past his drinks/dinner and the "boys" watched me. I smiled and took my luggage to "my" room. Then I came down for a drink and a bite to eat. He got to watch me the whole time. And the clients did too. Little did they know.

He headed toward the bathroom. I followed him. We snuck a kiss.

"How long are you going to be with these guys?" I asked. "I'll be upstairs waiting."

We always respected our jobs and business. I got a glass of Cabernet to go and headed to his room. I sent an email to my internal partner at work that I missed my flight and would be on the morning flight home from Atlanta.

When Bertrand finally came up, I was naked except for my shoes. Black patent leather high heels. I wore them even going through airports. I always wear heels.

"Took you long enough," I teased as he undressed and joined me on the bed.

"You are so bad," he said.

"And you love every minute of it."

We laughed and had a great night. He told me about the comments from the guys watching me. And having to keep a straight face knowing I was upstairs waiting in his bed.

I got up at 4:30 a.m. to catch my flight. Took a shower. I stood by the bed in my thong underwear and bra and asked if I should put on coffee for him. He said no, and sweetly kissed my exposed stomach as I got dressed.

"Go back to sleep," I said as I closed the door to pick up the shuttle. Still smiling even if it was stupid early.

ANOTHER SECRET LOVER

For the most part, rules are just guidelines. I found myself at the Atlanta airport. Again. It had been a long week. Thursday night and heading home. Time to board.

I always people watch as I'm standing at the gate. I pick out the road warriors, vacationers, families; admire the nice outfits, shoes, and cute guys.

I was dressed in my "uniform" — a black pantsuit with a maroon pinstripe and maroon blouse underneath. I was at the gate with my black roller bag and my purse filled with what was left of my work materials. I looked over the people.

First class lined up. Road warriors next. You want to make sure you can get your bag in the overhead bin and not have to check it.

Then I spot this really good-looking man. Tall. Scruffy beard. Great arms, strong, full sleeve of ink on one arm. He was wearing a T-shirt and work pants. Baseball cap. Damn sexy. I looked away. After a long week, I wasn't feeling sexy. Not as bad as the "cat dragged me in" bad, but not your prettiest.

I looked over again and smiled. He was looking at me too. The third time I glanced over, he was gone. That's because he was standing behind me.

"If I knew the flight was delayed, I would have had another beer," he said to me.

I turned around.

"And I would have had another glass of cab," I said. "Heading home?"

"No, going to help my parents move in Ft. Lauderdale. You?"

"Yep." I'm thinking, *Bummer.*

We started to board. "That's me," I said as they called my group. Smiled at him again.

I threw my luggage in the overhead bin. I got settled in my aisle seat and watched for him to board. I was only a few rows back so I could see him as soon as he stepped on. He smiled at me when he got on the plane. A genuine smile. I smiled back.

Trying not to be obvious, I watched him go to his seat. He was in the back of the plane. I sent him a beer.

He insists that everyone knew. The flirting, the smiles. Certainly the flight attendants did. I thought we were being more subtle than that. We just met 15 minutes before. But I would have done the Mile High Club thing with him right then and there. Maybe that was hard to hide.

When I got off the plane, luggage in tow, I made a decision.

I waited for him. He seemed surprised to see me outside the gate.

"I wasn't sure how I was going to meet you again," he said.

"Hmmm." I smiled. "Problem solved."

We walked out together. Still making goo-goo eyes at each other.

"How long are you here?" I asked.

"Just the weekend, to help my parents," he said, a bit of disappointment in his voice.

"Do you need a ride?" I offered.

"No, my folks are picking me up."

"Well, I'm only 30 minutes from Ft. Lauderdale," I said. He was still standing next to me as the airport valet pulled up my car. "Here's my card and number if you get a chance."

I didn't hear from him that weekend. But the next week I did. He was back home in Charleston.

We started to text each other. We became friends. He said his situation at home wasn't great. He admitted to being married, semi-separated, young kids. Stressful job.

It became texting daily, usually early in the mornings to say hello. He got up at 4:20 and went to the gym and was at work by 7:00 a.m.

After a couple months we decided to meet in Georgia, where he had to be for a project.

His boss decided to go with him. So "no go" for me. I had already purchased my ticket. He couldn't take that risk. I understood, but it still sucked. I know he was bummed too and felt bad.

We decided to try again between Christmas and New Year's. We agreed to meet where he lived. I had time off and there was nothing going on at work. So I took a few days off and flew to Charleston.

I picked a hotel on the beach. It was raining. I went next door and grabbed some soup, then chilled in my room watching the stormy weather from my balcony. And trying not to think too much.

The next day I got up and put on a pair of cute black cargo-style jeans and a black sweater with short high-heeled booties. Checked my hair and makeup twice. My hair hates the rain.

He was coming at lunch time. I asked him what he wanted to eat and he didn't care. I guess that wasn't the point really.

I went downstairs before he arrived and got a miniature bottle of Pinot Grigio from the lobby marketplace. I downed it in one gulp. I was that kind of nervous. Even with all the texting, it's not the same as meeting him again in person.

He texted me right before he arrived. I gave him my room number.

The minute I opened the door to my room he took me into his arms. It was the biggest hug. He scooped me up and kissed me.

"I just left work and you look so nice," he said.

"Thank you. You are so sexy. How much time do you have for lunch?"

"I don't know. I didn't say anything. I just left."

I had ordered some subs delivered to the front desk.

The kisses didn't stop. He took my sweater off. Then I took his T-shirt off. Wow.

"I'm not sure how good this is going to be," he said. "I haven't had sex in at least eighteen months."

I took his chin in my hands. "It will be great. You're great."

Later that afternoon we were lying in bed together. I was nuzzled between his collarbone and his chin. Right in the "nook." He had this troubled look on his face.

"Are you okay?" I asked.

"I've never cheated on my wife."

He pulled me close.

"Are you sorry?" I asked, trying to gauge what was going on in his head.

"Not at all." He kissed my forehead.

"Let's eat," I suggested. I had them bring the food up and leave it at the door. I had ordered an Italian sub for him and tuna for me. Tuna, what was I thinking?

I threw on a T-shirt, the one I usually sleep in. He put his white boxer briefs on.

I couldn't help looking at him as we had lunch.

"Why are you looking at me that way?" he asked. "You've already seen me naked and had me."

After lunch he had to go back to work. He started to get dressed.

"No, no, no," I teased. "You told me you are not a 'one and done' man." I ordered him to get undressed. "Remember?"

"You are holding me to that?"

"Absolutely."

I headed home the next day.

Many years later we are still lovers now and then. Even better, we are friends. Life doesn't need to have a storybook ending. In fact, the real world is almost always better than the fairytale one.

I live in the real world. I like it here.

MR. RED FLAG

*Never ask a question you don't
want the answer to.*

The problem with the real world is the people who don't live in it but think they do. The people who live in their own reality and don't care about yours.

I met Mr. Red Flag on a dating app. Online dating is hell. Just too much bullshit. Ninety percent of the profiles are fake. Scammers looking for money. Five percent are just lying. If a guy says he's forty-five you can usually add twenty years. Or subtract twenty years for the guy who looks like a teenager but says he's forty-five. He's probably looking for an experience with an "older woman."

Three percent are scary. I had to use Urban Dictionary to understand some of the lingo. Unicorns. Pineapples. Eggplants. Peaches. That's how I learned what "pegging" means. Educational.

So basically that leaves about two percent as actual humans you'd want to meet in real life.

Mr. Red Flag and I totally hit it off at first. We started texting and talking every day. I enjoyed the intelligent conversation. Business, food, movies. The markets. You name it. He was charismatic.

I lived in Houston but traveled every week for work. He lived in Austin and worked as a custom welder all around Texas. I'd meet him when he was on a job.

I saw red flags from the beginning, though. Some things didn't add up. Timelines. Stories. Family. Marriages.

I told my bff that something just didn't seem right.

"Do you care?" she asked me.

"I don't think so, yet," I said. "But we'll see. I am a lot of things; stupid isn't one of them."

"Yeah, see how it goes."

He called and texted me all the time. He would send me pictures of him working. Pictures of him cooking dinner. I would help him when he had investment questions. We would talk during the day, at night. While he was brushing his teeth. When he passed a kidney stone. When he was clothes shopping.

Still, something just didn't add up. I kept thinking he had a wife, a girlfriend, a boyfriend, a farm animal? Who knows.

But if that was the case, how could he spend so much time texting and talking to me?

Three things to know:

1. I couldn't come to his place because he shared it with his army buddy living in the guesthouse. He was saving up to buy a house. Not having women over was a rule because the roommate had young daughters. Red flag.

2. I couldn't wear perfume because he has a sensitive nose. Red flag.

3. He never bought me a gift. Not even a card. Red flag.

This relationship went on for about three years. I let it, so that's on me. I loved him, and he loved me. I know that. He said he was getting burned out in Austin. We talked about moving in together of sorts. Half in Houston, half in Dallas. The "M" word came up. Marriage.

You know what happens next.

He started to dabble in meme stocks. I told him it was a bad idea and his expectations were unrealistic. And he was an idiot for trusting advice from the folks on websites.

He originally lost very little money and made some money. He was just playing around.

Then he really fucked up and blew a $25k deposit from a client, trading meme stocks. I had told him that it was a bad trade and it was not his money to lose.

He said he would figure it out.

"I thought I would never have to do this and you told me not to, but I lost the money, and I need to buy supplies to start this job," he told me. "Can you loan me $37k? It's a big job. Cost of lumber is up, and I need other supplies."

Money is money. If you ever lend it, assume you will never get it back. A lesson I already learned the hard way. My mind was reeling from him asking me for that much. Deep down I knew he was lying to me.

"I will need some additional information to even think about a loan," I told him. "What's to say you don't blow it on trading stocks again instead of doing this job?"

I called Bertrand. I knew I could count on him for a sanity check.

"Hire a PI," he said. "You always had red flags."

I decided to stall. Mr. Red Flag was pushing me for the money. I told him that I needed a copy of his driver's license and social security card, and banking information.

"There is no loan without it," I said.

"I will get it to you when we do the loan paperwork," he promised.

No, hell no. That is what my brain was screaming.

I found a great woman-owned private investigation company in Austin. Not everything is on the internet. I know; I had googled Mr. Red Flag and nothing came up.

She had reports ready in a matter of hours. First thing, it didn't show any military service. He said he was in the Army. Joined at eighteen. There were some tickets and minor arrests. Liens from business clients. *Great, this is getting better by the minute.* I was pretty sure at this point nothing he said was true.

She put a person outside her house. That's right, *her* house. The woman he lived with. They sent me a picture of his truck and her car in the driveway.

I texted the picture of the house where he lived with his girlfriend with their cars in the front. Specialty license tag, so no denying it.

"You have someone outside my house?" were the first words out of his mouth when he immediately called me.

"You mean Diane's house?" I asked him. "Oh, and I called her. At her office." I did that on purpose. I could have called her cell number that the PI gave me. But I thought calling the office would ensure I got a call back.

"I fucking hate you right now," he said.

"Gotta go," I told him. "She's on the other line." I had googled her too. She was cute and successful. At least he has good taste.

Diane and I had a nice chat about what he had been up to for three years with me. I had too much information for her not to know I was telling the truth.

He lost his home, her, and me in a matter of minutes. It felt great. Even if my heart was breaking.

"I don't have any money. I have like $700 and she kicked me out," he said when he called me back.

"That must suck," I said. "Not my problem."

"She's not going to take me back."

"Neither am I."

I was mad. Really mad. I hate Facebook, I hate social media. Period. But I posted, with his full name, that he was a lying, cheating piece of shit of a human being and connected it to his company somehow.

A couple days later I got a message from a random girl on Facebook.

"I don't do Facebook," I wrote back. "Text me."

As soon as I gave her my number she asked if she could call. Turns out her friend was also dating Mr. Red Flag.

"I always knew there was something wrong about him," she said. "Will you talk to my friend?"

"Absolutely."

I told the gal's friend everything. The lies he told us all. Diane in Austin and me in Houston and her in Dallas. Her story was just like mine. He had been seeing her less than a year. She had kids. He spent Christmas with them.

Who has the time to call, text, and send pictures to three women every day? kept going through my mind.

Months passed. I moved on. I updated my dating profile. Then he showed up in my queue. My heart could not take it. I felt stupid. I felt hurt. I was angry beyond words. Delete.

Sometime after that I needed a handyman, so I went to look on Thumbtack. So of course handyman ads started popping up in my emails, including one promoting his company. Days later, he shows up on Thumbtack itself. Two punches in a row. Good thing I am tough. I had a hole in my heart, but it would heal.

Love and loss are hard. Betrayal can be even harder. You will survive. I know.

THE FISH TANK AND
THE TOASTER

have survived more than my fair share of heartbreak. Past, present, and probably yet to come. Other people come and go. They key is not quitting on yourself.

Husband #1 asked for a divorce early one Sunday morning as we were watching Wimbledon.

I had been hired by Dean Witter and was supposed to be spending my time studying for the exam to be a financial advisor. But my boss made me work full time as an assistant to two advisors. I would study late into the night. I found out later the other trainees got to spend their time in the office studying.

It was a week before my exam. I was about to turn thirty and my entire life felt like it was in the balance. If you didn't pass the exam you didn't get to come back. There was no job for you. They mailed you any of your belongings you left in the office.

I didn't meet the criteria for the position. I don't have a college degree, and that was mandatory. But what I did have was nine years' experience doing sales in leasing and financing, and the sales manager liked me, even though he'd often remind me he was doing me a favor.

"You couldn't wait a week?" I asked husband #1.

I had changed. Over the years I grew up and had real jobs. He wanted to be a poolman and be done by early afternoon then get stoned or drink beer. That is all he wanted in life.

He still wanted to hang out at the beach and play frisbee with his friends. He wanted me to be the seventeen-year-old girl that he met on the beach.

I wasn't that person anymore.

The truth is I didn't want to be married to him either. He asked for the toaster and the fish tank. That is all he wanted out of our twelve-year relationship and seven-year marriage.

Done. I let him stay for a month to get things in order. It was probably the easiest divorce ever.

I used my office computer to print out the divorce papers. I mailed them to him with a self-addressed envelope and stamp and "sign here" stickies. He didn't even have to show up. A friend went with me to the courthouse to finalize it.

I passed the exam with an 84. I had a new career and my new life was about to begin.

PART 5

WORK HARD, PLAY HARD

SELLING TYPEWRITER RIBBON OVER THE PHONE

My first job in LA was selling typewriter ribbon over the phone. Yep, typewriter ribbon. It was generic ribbon, not name brand. *Just as good, with free shipping* was our main selling point.

It was not much of an interview. Basically, can you open a phone book, can you dial a phone, can you read a script? If you answered yes to at least two of those questions, you were hired.

It paid cash weekly. The office was in Burbank. Two rooms with a handful of desks and bookshelf after bookshelf full of phone books. Flickering fluorescent lights. Ugly old mustard-brown industrial carpeting. The whole place smelled faintly of mildew.

The two owners, Keith and Dylan, were in their late twenties and part-time rockstars. Keith was about 5' 10" with dark hair and Dylan was 6' and blond. Both had the '80s hair and dressed the part for LA at the time.

We started at 6:00 a.m. so we could make calls to the East Coast. The day would end at noon. It was a motley crew. Chris was living down the street in his van. Bryce had a family and had lost his job, he was just trying to survive. Clair, who was really good on the phone, was about eight months pregnant. She was nice and would win a lot of the daily contests. That was usually about $100 cash. At least until I came along.

The training consisted of Dylan letting you pick a random number from the phone book and see if he could make a sale "on the spot." He was beyond good. We sold cases of ribbon to CPA firms, law firms, and medical offices. Anyone who did a lot of typing. You pretty much had to be able to close if you got someone on the phone. There was no follow-up.

You learned a lot about rejection, overcoming obstacles, and staying focused on the goal: money.

The pitch started with *I am calling about the ribbon you are currently using in your IBM Selectric typewriters.* Next we asked: *How many Selectrics do you have in the office?* The odds were about 90 to 10 that they had at least one if not hundreds. *How much ribbon do you go through in a month?* And went from there.

If you made a sale, Dylan would confirm the order and you would get paid at the end of the week on your orders.

A lot of people would come and go and last about a week, maybe two.

"Tomorrow is Keith's birthday," Dylan said one day to all of us. "I have a surprise for him when we shut down at noon. Feel free to stay for cake."

Two girls came in for interviews at 11:45 the next day. They didn't look like anyone applying for a job selling typewriter ribbon. They went into Keith's office and he shut the door. They were both strippers. I know a stripper when I see one.

After about 30 minutes the door opened and the scantily dressed ladies emerged.

"Nice surprise, Dyl," Keith grinned. The girls stayed to eat cake with everyone.

There were some days Dylan and Keith didn't show up at all. We would sit outside the building for a while and then go home.

My high school friend Gabby and her friend, Cheryl, decided to come visit us in California. They had become friends at a bar back in Florida. Husband #1 and I lived in a one-bedroom in an uptight building. Full of old farts and a lot of rules. We were already hiding our cat. I let the manager know we had friends coming for a visit.

Cheryl and Gabby arrived and they were in vacation mode. We had jobs. Not a good combination. After a few weeks, they were still staying with us. Offered nothing toward rent or food, slept all day and partied all night. That didn't sit well with the neighbors.

"You guys got to tone it down," I told them. "The manager is bitching at me."

"Yeah, no problem," they shrugged.

A few nights later, I heard Gabby and Cheryl come home around 3:00 a.m. They ate two boxes of macaroni and cheese, a can of tuna, and a can of tomato soup. That was all the food we had left until payday. They left a mess in the kitchen.

That's when I knew that enough was enough.

"The manager is saying the neighbors are complaining again," I lied. "We can't afford to lose our apartment."

They headed home a few days later.

I may have just been selling typewriter ribbon over the phone, but I'd moved myself to a new state and was working my ass off. I was learning my true friends would be the ones who were willing to work hard so they could play hard. I had been good at making my own money since I was sixteen and no one — not even a friend — was going to take advantage of me.

I will never be a doormat.

THE CLASS THEY WILL
NEVER FORGET

ast forward to 1993. After passing your test to become a financial advisor at Dean Witter you go to NYC for a month of training. My divorce wasn't yet final but husband #1 had already moved back to the Panhandle. I got a friend to cat sit and off I went.

Our classes were on the seventy-fourth floor of the World Trade Center. Previous classes got to stay at the Vista Hotel in Tower Two. We couldn't stay there because of the bombing earlier that year. Dean Witter put us up in a budget hotel across from Madison Square Garden. Dated. Smoke-filled curtains. Two people to a room, a small kitchenette. We took the subway from Penn Station to lower Manhattan every day.

My roommate had never been out of South Carolina. Never been on a plane. Every time she opened her mouth people would stare at her with her bright red hair and deep southern accent.

We sat in alphabetical order for the month. Next to the same people every day. One hundred guys and thirteen girls.

The firm only gave us a few hundred dollars to live on for the entire month. Some folks went through that the first week. Not me.

"Let's have a little dinner party," I suggested to my roommate one day.

"Invite a couple friends over? Sure, I'm in," she said.

It became a fifteen-person dinner party. Bring your own plate. Standing room only. Our beds became both chairs and tables. Some people sat on the floor. We went to the bodega around the corner, picked up some chicken, potatoes, and frozen peas. More food showed up. Pasta salad. Plenty of booze.

We were supposed to work at night, making calls to build a pipeline of potential clients. Practice what we were learning. Some folks went home on our weekends off. I couldn't afford to. Neither could my roommate. A group of us checked out the city on the cheap. Chinatown, Little Italy, the Met. I had never been to a museum like that before. I fell in love with art. It felt like a whole new world was opening its doors to me.

A couple weeks into the training it was Halloween. It also happened to be the night of the President's Reception. A group of us decided to go in togas. Seemed like a good idea at the time. It was Halloween after all. Me and a couple others designed the togas using the sheets off our beds. Someone picked up fake foliage for our headdresses. It was supposed to be a somewhat formal event and let's just say we missed the memo. The higher-ups were not amused.

After the reception a few of us decided to go to the parade. We walked blocks and blocks all over the city in our togas looking for the parade. It was somewhere in midtown. Well shit, we never found it. How do you not find a parade?

Two of the guys and I gave up and decided to take a taxi back to the hotel. One of them was a guy I had, well, hooked up with a couple of weeks into the training. He was drunk and being a real asshole.

"I can't *stand* the sound of your voice," he said.

That sent me over the edge.

"Cool it," the taxi driver warned.

I reached across the backseat. The asshole caught my right cross. First time I hauled off and hit someone.

The taxi driver threw us out. The three of us got to the hotel somehow. Still wearing our togas. It would be morning soon. Class would be starting in a couple hours. We had no sheets on our beds, we were wearing them.

We showed up to class freshly showered in actual clothes. The training center was in a buzz that morning. I got a couple of *looks*.

The asshole had a black eye and a small cut. Rumor was he tried to hit on me. I went with that. Don't ask. Don't tell.

NY PIZZA
TAXI

His 6' 4" ass got cold-cocked by a 5' 4" chick. He had to look at me for the next couple of weeks. His last name starts with F. Right next to G. Alphabetical order.

Years later, I ran into a young advisor doing a training seminar and THE "training class" came up in conversation.

"How long have you been in the business?" she asked.

"Since '93," I said.

"Did you ever hear about the class that showed up at the President's Reception in *togas*?"

I looked at her with a knowing grin.

"It was more fun than you could imagine."

THE INTERVIEW

Other people see you differently
than you see yourself.

Dean Witter wasn't the only time I didn't meet the criteria for the job I ended up getting. When I applied to be a rep for an asset manager, I had no clue what I was doing. I just knew I didn't like being a financial advisor.

I had always worked with other business professionals. I was not used to working with Ma and Pa Kettle. The public. And we are talking mostly elderly people who came in with handwritten notes on when their dividend checks should arrive.

Sometimes even if you don't know exactly what you want, knowing what you *don't* want is equally important.

I was working for Morgan Stanley. They had merged with Dean Witter a few years after I started. My office was in downtown Ft. Lauderdale. I had clients who would never venture into the city. So I went to them. I would travel west toward Plantation, where the branch manager would let me use his office to meet with clients.

One evening after I had met my last client for the day (they of course had to be home before the early bird special), I struck up a conversation with the branch manager.

"How's it going?" he asked.

I was honest.

"Well, dealing with John Q. Public just isn't me."

"Ah. Well, I know a money manager in West Palm Beach who is looking for representatives. Charles. He's literally written a book on investing. You should give his firm a call."

Without waiting for me to respond, he picked up the phone. "They're probably still there."

Sure enough, he got one of the top portfolio managers on the line.

"I've got this girl in my office," he said. "She's licensed, she's done sales in the past . . . you should talk to her."

The very next week I had my first interview with Charles's company. I wore my best suit — actually my *only* nice suit. Business professional, except it was melon in color. I had bright orange shoes to match. And of course, pantyhose. Welcome to being a woman in the brokerage industry in the '90s.

The first interviews went well. Next, I had to interview with all the partners. Nine people. Separately. I guess I just hoped for the best. I told myself I was good enough.

Charles liked me. He was in the Air Force when he was young. I shared that I was an Air Force brat. There's something about being in the military that instantly makes you family. He'd moved to Florida and started his own firm. He loved college football. So do I.

I found out later that the fact he talked to me for an hour was a shock to everyone. He usually only interviewed people for 15 minutes, max.

Before they would hire me, they wanted to see how I presented. Okay. I could speak on anything. I had nothing to lose. I went home and read Charles's book and studied all the firm's marketing materials.

The next week I presented to a conference room full of people from the office. I set up the presentation as if I was already doing the job.

You pretend that you are all advisors that I will be working with, I instructed the room.

I had no notes. I had learned it. Cold. I memorized it over the weekend. Quite frankly, I nailed it. I knew it.

When I finished I was told by Melanie, who was Charles's right hand, that I made one mistake.

Melanie would become CEO some years later. Even back when I interviewed she was already pretty much running the place. She's someone who is always multitasking, brings her paperwork into meetings, generally doesn't pay attention during presentations.

But she *had* been paying attention. I had said the firm had ten billion in current assets. Melanie informed me it was actually only one billion.

"Well," I said with a straight face and a smile in my eyes, *"you haven't hired me yet."*

At that point I was pretty sure that got me the job.

She told me after I started how surprised people were that I delivered that presentation with such confidence.

"When you walked in the first time all the men were drooling," she said. *Seriously, guys,* she had said to them.

I was surprised. I have never seen myself that way.

"About five minutes into your presentation," she said, "I realized, *Holy shit, this chick has got it.*"

I admitted to her that I had nothing to lose. I just went for it.

"Well," she said, "cheers to the next nine billion."

LIFE AFTER HOT DOGS

If one job doesn't pay the bills,
get a second job.

When you feel like you have nothing to lose, you are free to take more chances. I have never been afraid to put myself out there and see the person I could be. The path ahead isn't always clear and may not lead to the destination you hoped. But as long as you are learning and growing along the way, it's probably the right path.

Back when I was in my early twenties and working as an assistant to the sales team for Peter's (Mr. Hot Dog's) company in southern California, I made a point to have a conversation with him on one of his visits from Boston. I wanted to make more of a difference. I wanted to be important. I wanted to be successful.

So I invited him to lunch.

"I'm pretty sure there's a place down the street where we could get a hot dog," I laughed.

By this time it was a running joke. Hot dogs for lunch.

I didn't waste much time getting right to it. "How can I gain more authority over decisions being made for clients?" I asked him.

He knew what I was asking. I wanted more.

"Okay," he said, "here's what I want you to do for me to consider that."

He told me to look at 100 random existing accounts and note my analysis of the decision made in each case.

"Tell me what you would have recommended," he said.

That Friday I printed out 100 random accounts and took them home. I spent the weekend going through them. All of them. I have never been afraid to work for what I want.

I looked at their other credit, both for the business and the clients personally. What decision would I have made based on the data we had received? Are they a good risk? It was both an art and science.

I FedExed the finished files to Peter first thing Monday morning. He was already back in Boston.

He messaged me as soon as the package arrived. "You did *all that* over the weekend?"

I don't think he was entirely surprised.

"You said to demonstrate how I would have evaluated each account and what my credit decision would have been. That is what I did."

"Let me review all this," he said. "I'll get back to you."

Soon afterward I got the approval to grant up to $50,000 of credit for potential clients. I always wondered if Peter actually looked at the work or if the fact that I did it over the weekend said enough about my commitment to earning what I wanted. I never asked.

One late Friday afternoon we had a "rush" request from a representative. Sometimes sales reps try to push things through on Friday afternoons or at the end of a month. Goals and commissions are on the line.

I was the only one left at the office. My first decision. It was a bad credit risk.

"I can't approve this application," I told the rep. "You're welcome to have a senior manager evaluate it on Monday." I could feel the frustration on the other end of the phone. But I didn't give in.

The evaluation by the senior credit manager confirmed my decision. It was a good decision. I wasn't afraid to stand by what I knew. Trust yourself. Don't be afraid.

And never miss an opportunity to go out for a hot dog with your boss.

THE CORPORATE
ATTORNEY PART ONE

I worked my way up to becoming a collections rep for Peter's company. I didn't know that meant I was going to end up doing legal stuff. But sometimes accounts would get to the point where they were beyond what we could solve. That meant taking legal action.

I was introduced to Landon, our corporate attorney. I was on the job just a couple months when he first walked into our office in Irvine. Oh boy. He was cute and young, probably only a few years older than me. He noticed me just as quickly. I thought, *Please tell me he's the attorney.*

I am a firm believer in chemistry, the vibe you get from people when you meet them. It can be positive or negative. Then there is the *damn* factor. There was no denying that he was *hot*.

Landon and I met at his office to discuss an upcoming case. It was decided to take it to small claims. Attorneys are not allowed to be present in small claims court. So it was just going to be me. I don't even have a college degree. Landon was coaching me on how it would proceed.

That turned into lunch.

I had never yet seen how the "other half" lived. A nice restaurant overlooking the water. A two-hour lunch. The bill was more than what I spent in a week on groceries. It was the first time I understood the term "working lunch."

I had the spinach salad with warm bacon dressing and a glass of Chardonnay. *People live like this.* It was a whole new world to me. I tried to pretend it was normal. Hold your head high. Smile. Comment on how lovely the restaurant is.

I didn't look like the other guests. I had cheap plain clothes and synthetic black pumps. We talked about the case, about him being a lawyer and the son of a senator. He talked about playing baseball in college. I told him about my years as a gymnast. Our worlds were so far apart but they were close in different ways.

Damn.

It was a rare rainy day in Southern California. Landon and I ended up playing in the rain. Laughing, talking, splashing in the puddles. Me hogging the umbrella. It was like a scene from an old-school romantic comedy. We went back to his office building so I could pick up my car and go back to work. I went up to his office, where I'd left my keys. A little wet from the rain.

Then out of the blue his dad stopped by. He was dressed in an expensive suit and had a commanding presence.

Landon politely introduced me. "This is Stephanie; she does collections for our client."

The two of them walked into the reception area for a minute. My heart sank as I overheard a bit of the conversation, specifically his dad's comment: *She looks like she would be "discreet."*

I took my first case to court. The client didn't owe a lot of money. To me, not the point. You signed a contract, so you owe the money. The client tried to settle before court. "No" was my answer. I had tried everything to work it out with him before we got to court.

It was a major rush, standing before the judge, going through the facts, presenting the case. I would have been a good lawyer.

Landon was so proud of me when I told him that we won and that I nailed it.

"Come hang out on my parents' yacht with me," he said.

"I have to work today, remember."

"Don't go back to work. You deserve it."

I have a stupid work ethic. I felt guilty taking a long lunch. I went back to the office. Only later would I understand that in the business world celebrating a win is acceptable. The company would have understood. I would have to learn to celebrate and reward myself for my successes. My brain just wasn't wired that way.

There was great chemistry between us. He was married and so was I. We would meet again on cases. More lunches.

Landon's dad was wrong. We weren't having an affair. But I kept his contact in my phone. You never know when you might need the number of a good attorney.

I'LL SLEEP WHEN I DIE

have always said that I'll sleep when I die. One weekend tested that for sure.

My friend Josephine and I worked together and went through breakups at the same time. Our families were a mess. Your friends can be family. The best part is you get to choose them.

One day Josephine and I took a break on the steps outside our office.

"Want to run the 5K with me for breast cancer awareness?" she asked out of the blue.

"Sure, I'm in."

I worked out at least once a week boxing and kickboxing. But I don't like to run. In the days just before the event, we "trained" twice by taking a run from our office down along the water and over the bridge.

The weekend of the run started with me on a redeye home from California on Thursday night. The novel *Twilight* had recently been released and I picked a copy up at the airport to read on the flight. I am pretty sure I wanted a vampire

or a wolf as a boyfriend. For me, a book can be like a movie —
I have to see the end. I got no sleep on the plane. None.

My flight landed at 7:00 a.m. I had a conference call at
9:00. No time to shower. I did the call, did expense reports.
Worked through some other management stuff. Next thing I
knew it was 3:00 p.m. Shower.

So it was Friday night. No sleep yet. Across the street at
Mizner Park the band 3 Doors Down was in concert and I'd
invited some of our friends to come hear them.

I set up the bar and made some quick appetizers for
everyone. Of course, the party started at my house before the
concert, then we all walked across the street to listen to the
band. It's a really small venue, which is great for a concert. It
was outside, weather was nice. No seats. Not crazy crowded.
Real bathrooms. One of Josephine's friends bought us drinks.
Another friend bought me a T-shirt.

We all walked back and everyone took off for home. I had
to clean up. Tomorrow was only a few hours away. Oh, today.
It's 1:30 a.m.

The alarm went off at 5:30 but I was already awake. Time
to run a 5K. *How hard could it be,* I thought. A little more sleep
would have been nice, though.

I parked my car and walked to where the sign-in was at. I
put out a cigarette on my way to sign in.

Josephine was like, "Really? A smoke now?"

5k RUN
BREAST CANCER
BENEFIT
SIGN UP

"It's a run for breast cancer, not *lung* cancer," was my response.

Thank god for the sugar-free Red Bull I drank on the way. I kept thinking *5K, no problem.*

We ran together. And no, we didn't set any records. But we finished, no problem.

It was also Josephine's fortieth birthday. So of course we had planned a party for her that evening.

I grabbed my overnight bag from the car. Then we walked through the farmers market. Her place was only a block and a half away.

We picked up a couple of things. Olive oil, flowers, cheese.

"Tonight will be fun," I told her. "I know it's been a rough year. Let's not think about that. Just have fun."

"You betcha," she said. "Thank you for doing this."

I had booked the party at her building's common space. The guests started to arrive. We were all set. We had music playing, all the decorations were in place.

I didn't know most of her crazy friends. Her gay friends loved me. There was dancing, laughing, and stupid-picture-taking by everyone.

Then I had to clean up. Josephine stayed and helped. I have no idea what time it was. Hell, I didn't know what *day* it was.

She had a one-bedroom, so I finally crashed literally on her couch. I could have slept on the floor, or in a tub, on the balcony. It didn't matter at that point.

I woke up and had no clue where I was. Coffee. It's now Sunday morning and all this started on Thursday.

"Did you have fun last night?" I asked as I sat drinking coffee on Josephine's balcony and watching people walk their dogs.

"Absolutely," she said. "What a great day."

"I have to get home before I totally crash," I said.

I grabbed my bag and walked to the parking deck to my car. Time to make the 30-minute drive home. It'll be Monday morning soon.

I'll sleep when I die.

I'LL TAKE HIS NAME
TO THE GRAVE

The clubs in LA didn't get started until after 10:00 p.m. My roommate found a Chinese restaurant that would convert to an underground club on Thursday nights. They *only* played Springsteen. Even bootlegged recordings from his shows.

It was 1985 and the movie *St. Elmo's Fire* had come out that summer. One Thursday night I was wearing a bright yellow, tight-knit dress, hair all big à la Demi Moore's character "Jules." There happened to be some of the cast from the film at the club. No one was bothering anyone. It was just Springsteen and drinking and dancing.

The actor hit on me. I knew who he was but I wasn't going gaga over him like all the other girls in the club. We danced and drank Crown on the rocks. We chatted. He was a huge Springsteen fan.

The other girls in the bathroom were bitchy.

"You are his type . . . for tonight," one blonde sniped at me. She was definitely a wanna-be.

"And *you* are not," I shot back.

"It is really late, I'm going home," my roommate informed me. I was thinking, *Are you kidding me?*

"I need to go; she's my ride," I told him.

"I will get you a cab," he offered.

Just the response I was looking for. My roommate left, alone.

We closed the party down and ended up at the house of a guy whose dad was an executive at the Creative Artists Agency.

A hot tub, a guest room, and a taxi ride home.

Somehow, I ended up with his jean jacket and T-shirt.

I got home in time to shower before work.

The club got shut down shortly after.

So many people in LA are trying to be someone they aren't. I wasn't a wanna-be. I worked for a bank. I lived in the real world. And I wasn't going to kiss and tell all over town. But yes, he is that pretty in person.

THE GATE

Wherever I go, I seem to find my peeps or they find me. Anyone who isn't afraid to be a little bit different. Anyone willing to wear a toga made from bedsheets, sing karaoke at a dive bar, ride around a hotel parking lot in a shopping cart. It's all about chemistry.

I continued to find success in my career. Nearly three decades after my training in NYC I found myself working in sales for an asset management company in upstate New York. I was living in Houston and visited the home office twice a year.

One of the best people I worked with, Lucas, lived only seven miles away from me in Houston. Lucas is 6' 7" and his wife Rachel is probably 5' 10". They met in college.

When we weren't on the road, the three of us would do lunches, or dinners, or drinks, and maybe a dive bar together. Their house in Texas was the "fun" house. It was a big house in a nice neighborhood. Huge yard, beautiful pool. Gated driveway. They threw great parties and always had a well-stocked bar.

One of the first times we met for dinner I took an Uber because I don't believe in drinking and driving, even if it's just one drink. Lucas and Rachel pulled up in an Uber as well. At that moment I knew we'd be friends. You never know how the night might go.

Occasionally, our portfolio managers would come into town for meetings. They would go with us to do a meeting or two with clients while they were in town. Clients always appreciated getting to meet with them, since they were "the guys."

The portfolio managers don't get out much. They stay in the office, do research, and talk to the companies we invest in, or might be looking to invest in.

Matthew was like most portfolio managers and didn't travel much. He was an average-looking guy with a wife and young kids. He's one of those non-smokers who ends up smoking your cigarettes when he drinks too much.

On this particular visit to Houston, Matthew decided to stay with Lucas and Rachel. Rachel made dinner for us all. Salad, short ribs, herbed potatoes, and brussels sprouts.

I always bring something when I get invited to a party or dinner. It's only polite. I put together a cheese tray to snack on while we had wine before dinner.

We opened the first bottle of wine, a nice Cabernet from California. The second bottle was open even before dinner. We talked a little shop. The home office gossip. Sports, always. Sales, markets. We didn't get too deep.

"Cards?" Lucas suggested.

"All in," both Matthew and I chimed in. We played some game that I knew nothing about. It was getting late. I lay down and fell asleep on the coach.

My first meeting with Matthew and my clients was scheduled for nine the next morning, downtown. He was going to meet me there. Downtown from my house is only about a 20-minute drive through Memorial Park.

I woke up at 3:00 a.m. on the couch. A little crusty.

I ordered an Uber, walked out of the house to go meet the car. One minor problem, the wrought iron gate was closed. It had never been closed before because I usually left at a reasonable time. The ornate gate and cement walls attached to it must have been at least nine feet tall.

I couldn't get back in the house. I called Lucas and Rachel. No luck.

The Uber pulled up, but I was "jailed" in. I thought about trying to figure out how to get over the wall. The Uber driver looked at me like I was batshit crazy.

"I need to get home," I pleaded with him. "I have meetings in the morning."

He didn't say anything. He got out of his car and leaned against the gate just enough so I could squeeze through. Purse first and then me.

"You rock dude," I said. "Thank you so much."

I was home in fifteen minutes and slept for two hours.

I woke up as usual at 6:00 a.m., showered, slammed down a sugar-free Red Bull, put on my makeup, did my hair, and put on a black suit with black patent leather peep-toe shoes and matching jewelry.

Back at Lucas's, I found out later, "the boys" were having coffee and breakfast at 7:00 a.m.

"Fifty/fifty chance she doesn't make it on time," Matthew said.

Big laugh from Lucas. "One hundred percent guarantee she will be there early with bells on."

I was there before Matthew and fully prepared. He looked at me.

"Damn."

In our industry you have to be able to entertain, thrive without sleep, and make it look easy. It should be part of the interview process. It's part of the job.

Later that day I told Lucas about my escape at 3:00 a.m. I'm not sure how long it took him to stop laughing.

"For future reference," he said, "there's a big red button next to the door that opens the gate."

I laughed. "Well *that* would have been good to know."

PART 6

Just Give A Fuck

GET BUSY LIVING OR
GET BUSY DYING

I didn't know you aren't supposed to ship human remains via UPS. There's a lot we don't know about death until it's staring us in the face.

First of all, calls from unknown numbers are never good. For me, too often it meant *Hey Stephanie, can you bail me out of jail?*

My friends know not to bother me on Sunday afternoon during football season. So I let this Sunday afternoon call go to voicemail. Then I listened to the message.

I called the number back.

"Is this Stephanie Geller?" the voice on the other end of the phone asked me.

"Speaking."

It was the coroner in Denver.

That is when you swallow hard and feel what's coming next in the pit of your stomach.

"We see you are Reginald Burgher's power of attorney," she said matter-of-factly. "We wanted to let you know he passed away."

UPS STORE
RIP

On Thursday, just a few days before, I missed a call from Reggie. I was walking into a meeting so I texted that I would call him afterward. He never answered my calls after that. He was finicky that way. Such a drama queen.

I knew he was going in for outpatient surgery for his back. I had told him it was a bad idea. It was the last time he didn't listen to me. Now he was gone. His neighbor who had been watching his dog while he recuperated walked in and found Reggie dead on the floor next to his bed. His body was cold.

A week later I flew out to Denver to settle Reggie's affairs. His "estate" was an apartment filled with junk. Everything needed to be dealt with. Every drawer and closet and storage bin needed to be cleaned out. Furniture. Banking. His dog. Bills. An RV. His website. The logistics were overwhelming.

Per his wishes he was cremated. I picked out an urn for his ashes and called his mother to get her address. I didn't know what to do with the ashes of the man who saw me as his closest friend. The friend who literally trusted me with his life. And now with his death.

I put together a box with pictures of him and the doggies. He'd had professional portraits taken a few years back. He looked happy in them. Not like at the end. I put the urn in the box with the photos and sent it to his mother.

She called me immediately when the box was delivered.

"I didn't know you were shipping me *him*," was all she said.

THE CORPORATE ATTORNEY PART TWO

I seem to connect with people whose lives are as different as humanly possible from mine. I met Amy in LA when I was first hired at Peter's company. She was tall and thin, pretty, with brown hair in a fashionable short cut. *Elegant.* She had nice clothes and expensive shoes. She had a cute boyfriend named Ted who was in med school. She was in sales and drove a sports car.

I wanted to have a life like hers.

She didn't know how to do laundry. At twenty-seven. The housekeeper did that. But she was nice. Genuine. Different. We would joke about how different our lives were. And we now had the same job, splitting the LA market.

I had moved into sales and Amy, Ted, husband #1, and I went out on New Year's Eve to celebrate. We met at her apartment in Yorba Linda. My husband and I had never been to a neighborhood like that. We took my company car.

I was having really bad headaches. Stress headaches. I was prescribed Vicodin to try to help. I don't like taking pills, but I was desperate. It was New Year's Eve so everyone but me was drunk. So I drove.

"Take a right," Amy said as we headed back to her home.

"No, take the left then the right," Ted corrected her. They kept arguing as I was trying to find my way back to her apartment. We had only driven a couple blocks.

I got pulled over. The cops saw us come out of the bar. I explained I wasn't drinking. It didn't matter. They saw us come out of a bar.

This was before breathalyzers. They put me in the back of the police car and took me to jail for a urine test.

They let Ted drive home. He was hammered.

I don't like small spaces. At least I was in a cell by myself. I got released the next morning.

I was freaking out. Husband #1 was of NO help at all. He called the jail, still drunk, and insisted they didn't understand.

"She was the designated *drinker,*" he kept telling them.

I had all New Year's Day to think about it.

Now what am I going to do? I might have just ruined my career and my life. I was absolutely beside myself.

January 2nd. Back to work. I didn't tell anyone about the arrest. Amy didn't tell anyone either. I had come too far to crash and burn like this.

There had to be a solution. I called the corporate attorney. Landon. Soon enough it was all taken care of. His father thought *I* looked discreet. At the end of the day, Landon was the one who was discreet when I needed it the most.

THE PLACE WHERE
EVERYONE KNOWS
YOUR NAME

Decades after Landon introduced me to what it means to have a "working lunch," I have mastered the art of taking a break in the middle of the day to have a nice meal. This was even more important during the pandemic.

There's a great lunch spot a block and a half away from my condo in Houston. It's at one end of the best strip mall ever. Next to a boot repair store. They actually fixed a broken heel on one of my favorite pairs of shoes. Then there's the liquor store, the massage place, the UPS store, the pharmacy, the dry cleaners, and a dive bar at the other end. It rocks to have them all in one place.

I can walk there if it's nice out. I am always alone so I sit at the long bar that seats at least twenty; there are also a couple tables in the bar area. The bar's the first thing you see when you walk in. A chandelier hangs over the round table in the corner. Hardwood floors and teal accents give the place an upscale vibe.

The other regulars and I have become friends with Melody, the bartender. She is unbelievably nice and even more talkative. Some of them even followed her to this place from her last restaurant job. She is not afraid to put her life out there. All of us regulars have our "spots" at the bar where we can listen to her stories.

Melody tells her whole story to those of us she gets to know and trust. About her daughter, the ex-husband, the boy-friends. She drops F-bombs. She lets us taste any new con-coction she is working on. If there's a cute guy that is not a regular, I can always ask her if she knows him. Once, there was a good-looking guy that sat next to me. He went to the bathroom, so I asked her about him.

"That one's mine," she said with a laugh.

Sometimes I go there when I don't know what I want to eat. They have everything from burgers to lobster pasta to chargrilled oysters, fish tacos, and a crab and avocado appe-tizer served over dry ice so it comes out smoking.

"Mel, what am I hungry for today?" I'll ask her when I can't figure out what I want.

"I think the gumbo," she'll say.

One Wednesday I happened to sit next to two gentlemen. Handsome, intelligent, engaging. Maybe even a little sexy. Jon and Doug. They were ninety and ninety-one and had been friends for forty years. They were dressed in business casual.

Doug was a widower and Jon was still married. They had children and grandchildren. They always sat in the last two seats on the left side of the bar.

We started talking. They shared stories. Stories of life. Stories of business. Pictures of their families.

They decided we should share fish tacos and french fries. They had a cocktail, I had a glass of Pinot Grigio.

Brooke showed up. She worked next door.

Then Heather.

Heather was a pretty blonde and worked on her laptop while she ate lunch. She sat with us. They obviously knew her too. We had all chatted in the past.

Jon asked Melody, "Did Stephanie order a *fancy* wine?"

Melody smirked. "Does it matter, Jon?"

Jon and Doug refused to let me pay for anything.

As I was getting ready to leave I overheard a younger man ask Melody about our group.

"What *is* it with those old guys?"

She rolled her eyes. If you have to ask, you don't get it.

"We're usually here on Wednesdays around 11:45," Doug and Jon told me as they hugged me goodbye. I knew we would all be having lunch again.

"Keep my stool warm," I told them.

I always know how to find my peeps.

WHY ROAD WARRIORS NEVER WEAR WHITE

could write an entire book about living the life of a road warrior. Unless you have been a road warrior, it's hard to know what it's actually like. People think it's all first class and five-star hotels and fancy meals. It's not.

It's 4:30 a.m. wake-up calls. It's getting to your hotel at two in the morning with your first meeting at nine. It's often skipping lunch because you are hosting a meeting. The people in the meeting get lunch, but not you.

And then there are the happy hours. The dinners. It was nothing to work a 14- or 15-hour day. In heels. My number one rule for the road, especially when entertaining clients, was the "eleven o'clock" rule. The likelihood of damaging your reputation or screwing up your career increases after 11 p.m. That's why I invented the rule. Always leave the scene by eleven.

Another rule is never wear white when you travel. Go with black. You never know when you'll sit next to the lady with the baby, but when you do the baby will always throw up on you. You will inevitably have a meeting to go to as soon as you land, no time to change. Always carry baby wipes so you don't smell like baby puke. Believe me, it works.

Flying out of FLL on a Tuesday after a holiday weekend is never a good idea. One trip in particular had two guys who looked like they had not been to bed. The smell was a good clue. They threw up the entire flight. When someone pukes, I puke. I gave the guys my barf bag. I went and stood in the back as long as I could. The flight attendants understood what was going on. Even though the seatbelt light was on they just let me stand there.

One time I sat next to a guy who was green. Literally green. That bad. The good news: he slept almost the whole flight. He woke up about 30 minutes before we landed and went to the bathroom. He never came out. They had to land the plane with him still in the restroom. Security showed up. I wonder how that ended for him.

What else? Never check a bag. Create a packing list so you never have to worry that you forgot something. Always bring a cell phone charger and an extra pair of underwear. The airline will never offer this and might even say they "can't," but if your flight is canceled the airline can book you on another carrier. Give them the flight number and insist.

Finally, if your flight is delayed and you want to get a drink to kill time, go to the bar that's not directly in front of your gate. Or just have one drink. Otherwise they might not let you on the plane.

One of the best parts? When you show up at the hotel where you stay whenever you are in that town and they all know you by name.

Welcome back, Stephanie.

I wouldn't trade any of it for the world.

FOLLOW THE MONEY

I didn't know I was going to love life on the road. When I first got my job as a sales rep I knew nothing about the lifestyle that would mean. Schedule a trip to any given town. Often a city you have never been to. Set up all your meetings. Arrange your flights, hotel, car. Traffic, suburbs. New York. Boston. Alabama. You get lost. Every damn street in Atlanta is named Peachtree.

To be a sales rep in the investment management industry you need to be able to talk about market conditions, your products, and why someone should buy what you're selling. You educate yourself. You educate potential clients. You get to know all your competitors and they get to know you.

You entertain clients. "Relationship building" is what we called it. The clients were always men. The industry was ninety-two percent men. Not much has changed.

We took clients to happy hour, to dinner at the best restaurants in town. When I first started I didn't have a clue. I worked at Waffle House. A nice meal was when you ordered both steak *and* eggs. And don't forget the hash browns.

I tried not to look shocked the first time I looked at the menu and saw a steak for sixty dollars. I didn't spend that much on a whole week's worth of groceries.

"Which wine do you prefer?" I would ask the men. "What does it pair well with?"

I learned about food. I was hooked in no time. It was a crash course that I remember from a spinach salad at my first "working lunch" in 1987.

This was normal to them. How to order a steak. The difference between cuts. Why Oysters Rockefeller are so good. Why escargot is delicious. Funky things that taste great. I learned that I never had to look like a poor kid from the 'hood. I learned about wine. Why men pay for overpriced wine to show off. I learned how to spot a great wine at a reasonable price.

I was told to watch my budget but it was hard not to go over. *You have to spend money to make money.* I had an expense account that included travel, events, and all the dinners. It never went far enough. But the girls in accounts payable liked me. They knew I worked hard for every dollar.

Better to ask for forgiveness, not permission. The money kept coming in. Sales were beyond good wherever I went. Hundreds of millions of dollars.

Well, we know where Stephanie was in the last couple weeks was a running joke from the folks who worked with me.

"Follow the money," I would say with a smile.

I was working with a client in Alabama who didn't love what we did. I had been talking with him for three years. Then there was a market meltdown. The dot-com bubble burst. We got our asses kicked. It was brutal. I got a phone call from Alabama. I expected another beating. I was honest, I always have been.

I told him the truth. The truth about what was going on with the market. What my company thought. We knew a bubble when we saw it. It was just a matter of time.

The next day I got over 100 new accounts. They were from the guy in Alabama. The minimum amount for a new account was $100,000 at that time. Most of his were at least double that. Three years of work had finally paid off. Just being me had finally paid off. The folks in my company were freaking out. No one gets sales like that.

CHEMISTRY

Sales continued to grow. I got a little help. I had to take marketing materials on the road with me every week. The folders needed to be assembled. We'd build a production line in the office and stuff each folder with fact sheets and articles before I shoved everything in my luggage. Even one of the portfolio managers would pitch in. They were partners and got a percentage of everything I brought in.

Our biggest client did regional conferences. We paid to sponsor the events. Thank god that wasn't part of my budget. You sat through boring ass meetings and half the people played hooky on the golf courses.

My conference was in Atlanta. People signed up to go to your "dinner meeting." It was two managers to host and split the bill. It was pure networking. A dozen clients or prospective clients. It was a crap shoot who you would get. Turns out I hit the lottery.

The restaurant was one of the hottest places in Atlanta. You couldn't even get a reservation without knowing someone. It was old school. Red velvet chairs in the entrance.

Expensive linen tablecloths and napkins. White-gloved waiters and waitresses. We had a private room.

David, the other rep, was totally cool. He was experienced and sold a product that complimented mine. Rumor was his firm brought in $100 million in one day. One day.

We laughed about how we were a great combination. Sales but not selling. I got the team from Atlanta that I really liked. I got the gentleman from Birmingham. The rich redneck from Daytona Beach was also on my end of the table.

Chemistry. You can't force it. It either happens or it doesn't. The redneck from Daytona Beach was one of those guys who travels all over the world and thinks his shit doesn't stink. He wore a suit everywhere. Big personality. Big ego. The guy from Birmingham was the quiet reserved type. The team from Atlanta mostly observed and laughed, watching it all.

We shared about fourteen bottles of wine between the twelve of us. And the redneck from Daytona Beach ordered shots of Louis XIII. That is in a crystal bottle enclosed in glass and costs $100 a shot.

My company is going to shit when they see this bill, I thought.

As it turned out the redneck had been on a trip in Europe with the chef, so of course the chef had to come out from the kitchen to see us. The redneck was willing to pay for another round, that's $1,200. We declined, as most of us were already in the weeds.

We did get a complimentary dessert made just for us by the chef himself.

We got the bill. It was over six grand.

"That's my half?" I asked David.

"Yes."

Now for an after-dinner drink and cigars. That was downstairs in the lounge. More stories and another drink and everyone, including some of us girls, had a cigar.

Then we had to get back to the hotel. Call a cab for twelve. Thank god we got a station wagon. Pretty sure we broke a few laws. We all climbed in. A dozen drunks in a car. Thank god again, the hotel was close by. I have no idea who paid the taxi driver.

It was the type of next morning where you shower and you are still drunk from the night before and no one cares. I'm not sure if I washed the conditioner out of my hair. As it turned out, we were one of the first groups back to the hotel.

My clients from Atlanta had water, coffee, OJ, and Coke. You smile and laugh as you walk by. Take a seat in the back. Thankfully it was just a half day. We just had to pretend to pay attention for a few hours.

I got business from everyone at the table over the next few months. That expensive dinner brought in a ton of business. It was a good investment.

People from our table still talked about it years later. We had a blast. Chemistry.

MY GLASS IS FULL

ome say there are two types of people in this world: those who see their glass as half empty and those who see their glass as half full. I'm neither. The way I see it, if your glass is half full, it's also half empty. My glass is just full. It always has been.

My life is so much more than the sum of its parts. There are entire bookshelves worth of stories I *haven't* told here. Maybe someday. Some of them I'll take to the grave. But I have learned a thing or two along the way.

Growing up poor, I always watched every penny. I just never got over the feeling of being broke. No matter how much money you have, you get to decide what's necessary and what's not. At five years old I knew it was necessary to spend every cent in my piggy bank on the perfect gift for Eddie Spaghetti.

Over the years I invested in myself. In my career. I had to look professional. Ann Taylor, White House Black Market. Not Gucci. Not Louis Vuitton. Buy classic pieces. Early on, a Michael Kors purse or watch felt like a splurge.

Put money in the bank. Invest wisely. Always pay yourself first. Have more than a rainy day fund. Don't be afraid to dream of a different life for yourself.

It took me a long time to figure out how to "treat" myself. A nice dinner. A weekend getaway. A good bottle of wine. A real piece of jewelry.

"Do you have enough money to never worry about a bill?" a friend who came from a life like mine once asked. Both of our careers were starting to take off.

"Yes," I said. "I don't need to balance my checkbook anymore."

"It's crazy, right?" she said to me.

My first commission check was $315. I thought it was a fucking mistake. I worked harder. Then it was a few thousand. Then it was over $100,000 for three months of work. I got paid quarterly. I was making over $30,000 a month.

"You need to treat yourself every now and then," my friend told me.

"I don't know how to do that," I said. "I just know I never want to be poor again."

"You have accomplished so much," she said. "You don't see that?"

"No. I don't." I was honest. I never told the truth about how much I made to anyone. I'm not even sure I believed it myself.

I was a millionaire at forty. But I was also still the Waffle House waitress determined to win $50 selling the most steak and eggs. I may have never gotten my chance to compete in the Olympics, but I was always competing.

There are many ways to live a life. I've lived mine the only way I knew how. Work hard. Play hard. Follow the rules and know when to bend them. Love hard. Be generous. Be good to yourself. Take a chance. Ask for advice. Make mistakes. Apologize. Say thank you. Be real.

Basically, just give a fuck. Show up for your own badass life. And don't forget to carry your heart with you wherever you go.

ACKNOWLEDGMENTS

had no idea what I was doing when I started writing about my life. I just had the impulse to tell my stories. I want to give the utmost credit to the people who made this impulse real.

Credit goes to Sara Volle, my writing coach and editor. You are the person who made my stories better than I could have imagined. You talked me off the ledge when I wanted to throw in the towel and quit. You are so gifted and such a joy to work with.

To Susan Shankin, my publisher. You had the vision of what and who I am. And what this book could be. You made it beautiful and fun. I do not know how in the world you manage people like me every day and stay sane.

To Tim Kummerow, my illustrator. I could not have imagined working with someone so talented. You understood my crazy vision for these stories. Your illustrations are amazing and have added so much to this book.

To Julie Simpson, my copy editor. There were a couple of times I dreaded having you read my stories. I was scared, but you were positive with your feedback. You gave me hope. I am in awe of your attention to detail and the work you did on this book.

To my friends who shared so many of these adventures. It was a BLAST. Thank you for letting me be part of it.

To all my mentors and coaches. You know who you are. I will always be grateful for what you did for me. You took a chance on me, you believed in me. You helped me believe in me.

ABOUT THE AUTHOR

Stephanie Geller was born on Grand Forks Air Force Base in North Dakota. Her first move was two weeks later. As an "Air Force brat," she spent her childhood moving from place to place every few years with stints in Arizona, Florida, Montana, Germany, and Texas. After graduating from Niceville High School in the Panhandle of Florida, she moved to Los Angeles in 1983. There she got her start in the world of banking and finance.

In 1992 Stephanie became a financial advisor for Dean Witter. Four years later, she took her experience and success into the investment management industry, where she became a regional representative and eventually a national sales manager for Northern Trust Investment Management. In addition, she served as a partner in an asset management company and a majority partner for a cellular tower company covering the southeast United States.

Throughout her twenty-five-year career she has raised over a billion dollars in assets and has become a highly regarded public speaker. She was instrumental in creating marketing campaigns and white papers for her firm. As a member of the Investment Wealth Institute since 1996, Stephanie earned her Certified Investment Management Analyst (CIMA) designation from Wharton in 2001. She previously served on the National Conference Committee for the Investment Wealth Institute (IWI) and currently sits on the IWI's Ethics Committee. As a mentor at Northern Trust, she coached aspiring investment professionals.

Today, Stephanie owns her own consulting business. She loves good food and is a die-hard football fan, as well as a world traveler who has visited over thirty countries. She is currently single and lives on the fourteenth floor of a high-rise in Houston with her cat, Cody.